Editor
Mara Ellen Guckian

Editorial Project Manager
Ina Massler Levin, M.A.

Editor-in-Chief
Sharon Coan, M.S. Ed.

Illustrator
Renée Christine Yates

Cover Artist
Lesley Palmer

Art Coordinator
Kevin Barnes

Art Manager
CJae Froshay

Imaging
Alfred Lau
Ralph Olmedo, Jr.
Temo Parra
James Edward Grace

Product Manager
Phil Garcia

Publishers
Rachelle Cracchiolo, M.S. Ed.
Mary Dupuy Smith, M.S. Ed.

U.S. History Little Books
FAMOUS PEOPLE

★ Sixteen ready-to-assemble class projects featuring historic Americans

Authors

Brenda Strickland, M.S. and Pat Terrell Walker, M.A.

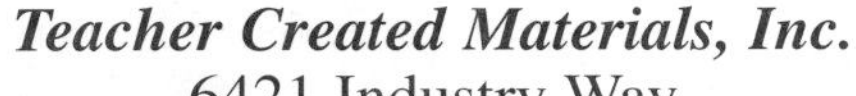

Teacher Created Materials, Inc.
6421 Industry Way
Westminster, CA 92683
www.teachercreated.com
ISBN-0-7439-3260-9

Table of Contents

Introduction

State requirements have become increasingly specific concerning the subject matter educators are expected to teach, and teachers have found it more and more difficult to find curriculum materials to meet students' needs. Age-appropriate history materials are needed. Many teachers are searching local libraries and the Web. What is often found is too advanced for the primary level.

The *U.S. History Little Books* series provides young children with simple, fact-filled books that they can make. The Little Books series focuses on important people, places, and events in United States history. Maps are included for each Little Book topic in order to give students a point of reference. A time line and a map of the United States are included to use for reference in the classroom.

Research indicates that children retain more information when they are personally involved in the learning process. Children will create folded books, layered books, pop-up books, and lift-tab books. In preparing the books, students will develop a variety of skills from following directions to cutting, coloring, and organizing. These books require their participation at many different levels.

Historical facts can come alive for a child who reads them aloud from a book he or she has helped to create. *U.S. History Little Books: Famous People* will increase students' knowledge of historical events, as well as developing small motor skills, reading abilities, and self-esteem.

This series uses the standards on the following page to help foster students' understanding of the history of the United States.

Introduction *(cont.)*

Social Studies Standards

The standards listed below are representative of those assigned to kindergarten through 3rd grade students throughout the country.

- Understands family life now and in the past, and family life in various places long ago

  Johnny Appleseed

- Understands the history of a local community and how communities in North America varied long ago

  Booker T. Washington *Harriet Tubman*

- Understands the people, events, problems, and ideas that were significant in creating the history of the nation

  Paul Revere *Lewis and Clark*
  Pocahontas *Booker T. Washington*
  George Washington *Martin Luther King, Jr.*

- Understands how democratic values came to be and how they have been exemplified by people, events, and symbols

  Susan B. Anthony *Booker T. Washington*
  George Washington *Jane Addams*
  Harriet Tubman *Martin Luther King, Jr.*
  Abraham Lincoln

- Understands the causes and nature of movements of large groups of people into and within the United States, now and long ago

  Lewis and Clark *Johnny Appleseed*
  Harriet Tubman *Christopher Columbus*

- Understands selected attributes and historical developments of societies in Africa, the Americas, Asia, and Europe

  Christopher Columbus

- Understands major discoveries in science and technology, some of their social and economic effects, and the major scientists and inventors responsible for them

  George Washington Carver *Benjamin Franklin*

- Understands the folklore and other cultural contributions from various regions of the United States and how they helped to form a national heritage

  Paul Revere *Pocahontas*
  Johnny Appleseed *George Washington*
  Jane Addams *Betsy Ross*
  Davy Crockett *Abraham Lincoln*

How to Use This Book

U.S. History Little Books: Famous People contains instructions and patterns for sixteen reproducible books primary students can create about historical figures. There are four different book styles—folded, layered, pop-up, and lift-tab. Students will find the variety exciting.

This book provides summarized biographies of each famous person as a reference. You should also gather some books from your library and read them to your students. Emphasize the most important points. You may want students to role-play some major events in the featured person's life.

Maps are included to give a geographical perspective. You may choose to make a transparency of one to share with the group, or you may make a hard copy for each student. If you do not have a wall map in the classroom, you may want to enlarge the enclosed maps. Encourage students to note the relationship between their home state and that of the historical figure.

The use of time lines is a way to organize or put events in order. Teachers can introduce the concept by discussing, with students, the events in their daily lives (i.e., get out of bed, eat breakfast, get dressed, go to school, etc.). From there, they can talk in terms of years instead of days (i.e., in what year they, their parents, or their siblings were born).

Some suggestions for using a time line include the following:

- Enlarge featured people cards on pages 8–10 and put them on a bulletin board. Highlight each person as he or she is studied.

- Place floor tape on a wall in the classroom. (Floor tape, like that used on gymnasium floors, will not pull paint off the wall.) Place the pictures from pages 8–10 on the time line in the appropriate order. Decide ahead of time if you wish to arrange the featured people by their birth dates or by the dates of their accomplishments.

- Run a clothesline across the classroom. Use clothespins to attach the pictures of the people from pages 8–10 along the line in the appropriate order. Add additional pictures or items where appropriate.

How to Use This Book *(cont.)*

The parent letter involves the parents in the educational process of their children. It will guide them on how to use the student-made books at home. This is a good way to encourage a strong home-school relationship.

Making books is an excellent culminating project following a unit of study. Children learn valuable reading and social skills and are proud to be able to read their own books to a parent or friend.

Decide whether you want students to create books individually, as part of a group activity, or as a class, then make the appropriate number of copies. Once students are familiar with the book-making process, they can learn to write their own innovative versions of newly acquired information.

Individual copies may be used. . . .

- in a reading group.
- as reading homework.
- as a study guide for standardized testing.
- as an extra activity to engage those students who complete their work early.

Group copies may be used . . .

- as a cooperative learning experience. (Each student prepares a page or two.)
- to add to the classroom library.

Parent Letter

Date:________________________

Dear Parents,

Today your child is bringing home a self-made book. This is just one of many he or she will create during the year. The books will be different in style but all will cover topics of importance in the history of the United States.

These books are for you to enjoy with your child. The books represent social science skills that each student is responsible for mastering. Encourage your child to "read" the book to you. Don't worry if all the words are not right or if the text is memorized. This is how reading begins. Celebrate what your child can do and the interest shown in wanting to read. Along with reading practice, these books can be used to review social studies topics before testing.

Your involvement in your child's academic life is critical to his or her success. The topics covered in the books are interesting and part of our history. You will enjoy reviewing these facts as your child learns about the United States.

Sincerely,

____

Teacher

Time Line

Christopher Columbus
1451–1506

Pocahontas
circa 1595–1617

Benjamin Franklin
1706–1790

George Washington
1732–1799

Paul Revere
1735–1818

Betsy Ross
1752–1836

Time Line *(cont.)*

Meriwether Lewis 1770–1838	**William Clark** 1774–1809	**Johnny Appleseed** 1774—circa 1845
Davy Crockett 1786–1836	**Abraham Lincoln** 1809–1865	**Susan B. Anthony** 1820–1906

Time Line *(cont.)*

Putting Together Folded Books

Materials

For each student you will need:

- a copy of each of the text pages
- a stapler
- a set of crayons or markers

Assembly Directions for a Folded Book

1. Color each page.* Trim the edges of the page.

2. Fold each sheet on the solid line.

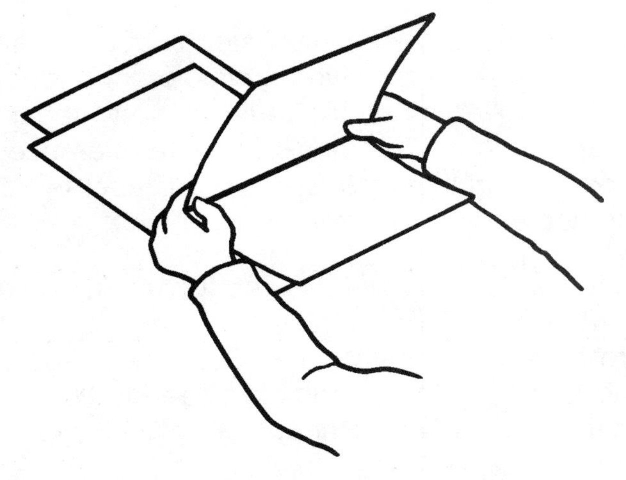

3. Stack the pages in numerical order.

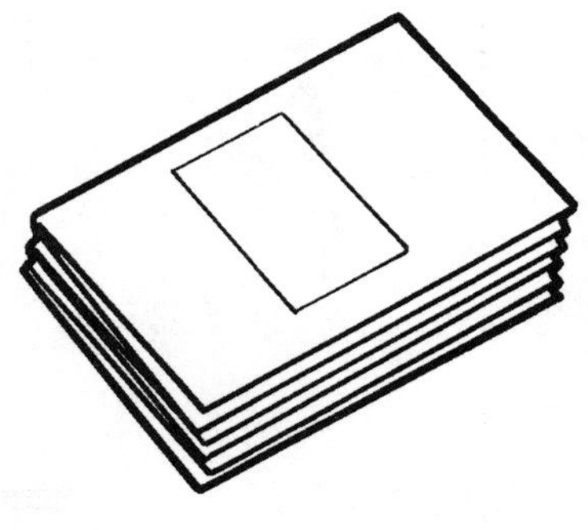

4. Staple down the left side of the booklet.

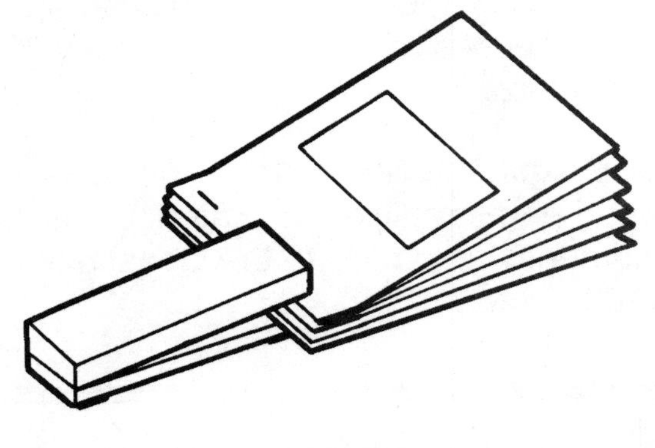

**The picture and text of half of the folded-book page is upside down. This is so that when the page is folded, stacked, and stapled, the book will read correctly.*

Susan B. Anthony

Susan Brownell Anthony was born February 15, 1820, in Adams, Massachusetts. Her parents were Quakers and raised Susan under the principle that men and women are equal. Beyond her Quaker home, however, the world had a different idea. Susan was allowed to go to school, but even there boys were allowed to do things that girls were not. This made Susan angry, and she did them anyway.

There was so much unfairness and inequality that Susan determined to do something to change the way the world worked. She devoted her life to fighting the injustice of women's inequality. She started in the schools by becoming a teacher. She taught all her students about these inequities.

Later, Susan became interested in banning alcohol, thinking that many people who drank alcohol became abusive and intolerant under its influence. Frustrated that because she was a woman she was not allowed to publicly speak out about such things, she began her organization, the Women's State Temperance Society of New York. During this time, she met Elizabeth Cady Stanton, another woman who shared her beliefs.

That women were not allowed to vote infuriated many women. In 1869, Susan B. Anthony and Elizabeth Cady Stanton formed the National Woman Suffrage Association. Their goal was to get a 19th amendment added to the Constitution of the United States. This amendment would give all women of the United States the right to vote.

Susan felt so strongly about her right to vote that she voted in the 1872 presidential election even though it was illegal for her to do so. Susan actively fought for women's rights for more than 50 years. She gave impassioned speeches, wrote persuasive books and articles, and courageously led women's rights organizations.

Susan B. Anthony died in 1906, never seeing one of her fondest dreams realized. It was not until 1920 that the 19th Amendment was added to the Constitution and women were allowed to vote.

19th Amendment

The right of the citizens of the United States to vote. Shall not be denied or abridged by the United States or by any state on account of sex.

Susan B. Anthony

Map Study

Susan B. Anthony was born in Adams, Massachusetts.

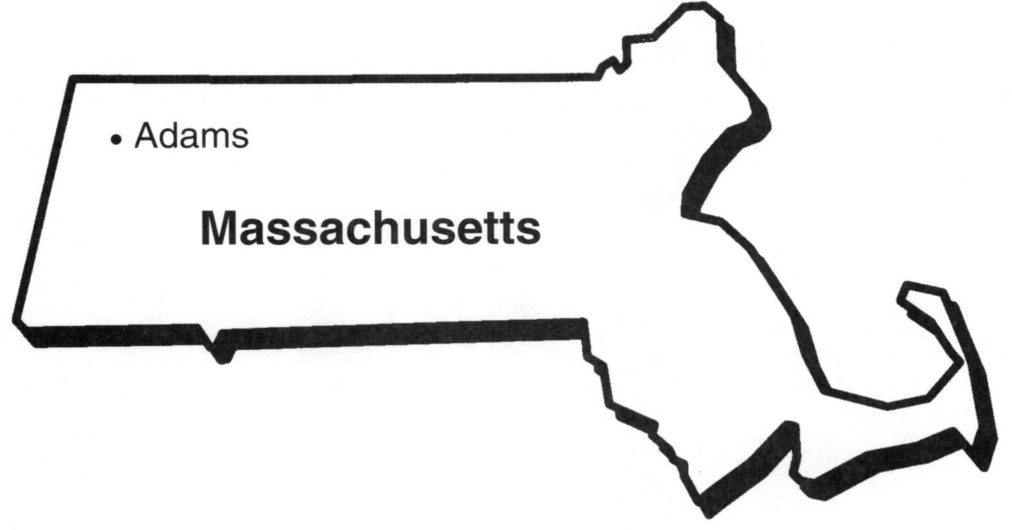

Susan B. Anthony was born in Adams, Massachusetts. As a child, she was angry that boys were allowed a better education than girls were.

1

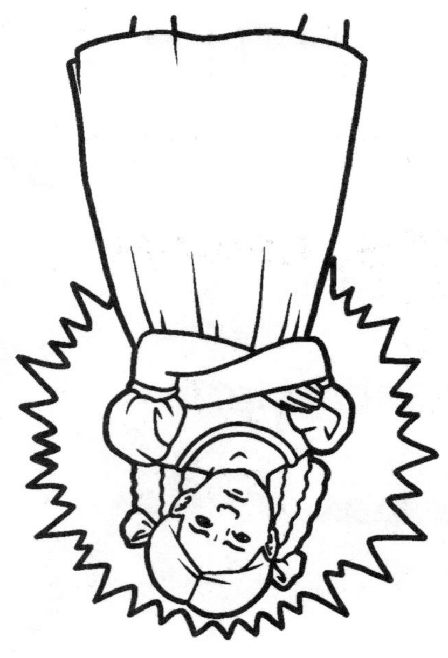

Susan B. Anthony

1820–1906

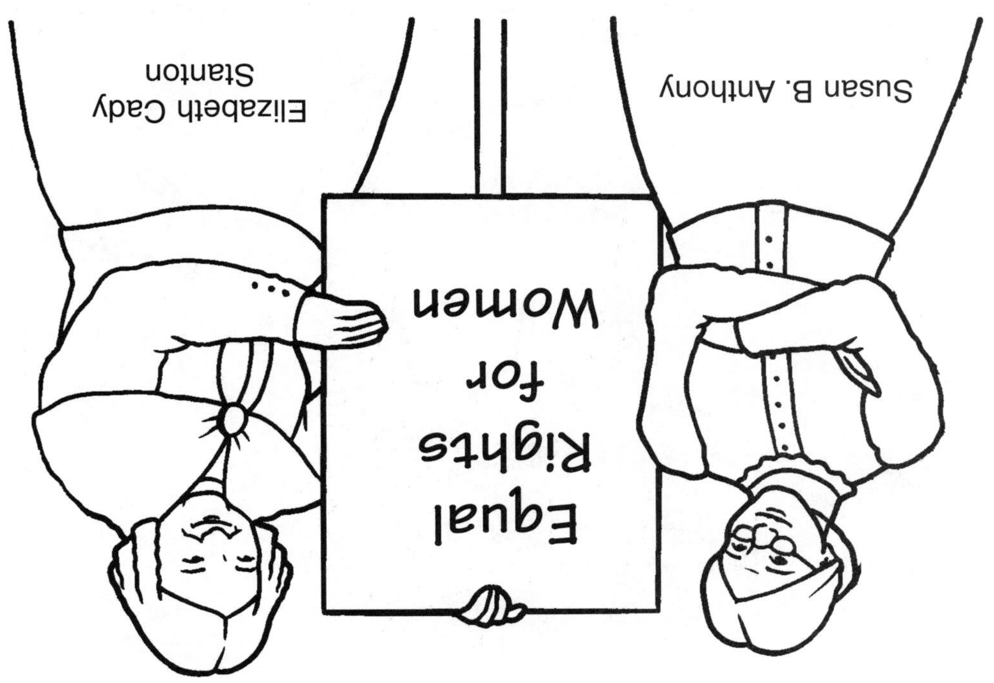

Susan believed that women should share equal rights with men.

3

When she became an adult, she taught school where she passed her ideas on to her students.

2

Susan B. Anthony fought to have laws changed to allow women the right to vote.

5

She was a suffragette.

4

Susan B. Anthony died before women gained the right to vote in 1920.

7

Susan B. Anthony and Carrie Burnham argued in court that women should have the right to vote.

6

She is honored on the 1979–81 and 1999 U.S. dollar coins.

8

Paul Revere

Paul Revere was born January 1, 1735. His father taught young Paul his trade, which was silversmithing. After the elder Revere died, Paul became Boston's leading silversmith. However, Paul Revere is even more famous for his part in the colonies' struggle to free themselves from British rule.

Paul Revere opposed the Stamp Act, which declared that the American colonists had to buy a British stamp for every piece of printed paper they used. This included newspapers, legal papers, business documents—even playing cards. Paul took part in the Boston Tea Party. He helped the Sons of Liberty to dump three shiploads of tea into Boston Harbor to protest the king of Britain's tax on imported English tea.

Paul also was a courier, or messenger. He rode on horseback many times to New York and Philadelphia to carry news of important events. He made his most famous ride on April 18, 1775. A group of American patriots had been gathering gunpowder and cannonballs and storing them in Concord, a little town about 20 miles outside of Boston.

When the British found out about the ammunition, they planned a raid on Concord to take it away. The patriots learned of the impending raid and knew they would have to act fast. They devised a system to let the colonists know how the British were going to attack. Someone would hang lanterns in the steeple of North Church—one lantern if the British came by land, two lanterns if they came by sea.

The British planned to take a shortcut across the Charles River and travel on to Concord by foot. As soon as the plan to cross the river was known, two lanterns were hung in the steeple. Paul Revere rowed across the Charles River—his oars wrapped with petticoats to muffle the sound—to Charlestown. There he mounted a waiting horse and raced toward Concord to alert the people that the British were coming. He warned people all along the route between Medford and Lexington. Because of the warning, the minutemen were ready. The *"shots heard 'round the world"* were fired. The American Revolution had begun.

Paul Revere

Map Study

Paul Revere's Ride started in Boston, Massachusetts. He intended to finish in Concord. However, he was intercepted by the British after leaving Lexington.

Paul Revere grew up in Boston, Massachusetts, when our country belonged to England. He had many brothers and sisters.

1

Paul Revere

1735–1818

He also made baby rattles, creamers, shoe buckles, and spoons.

3

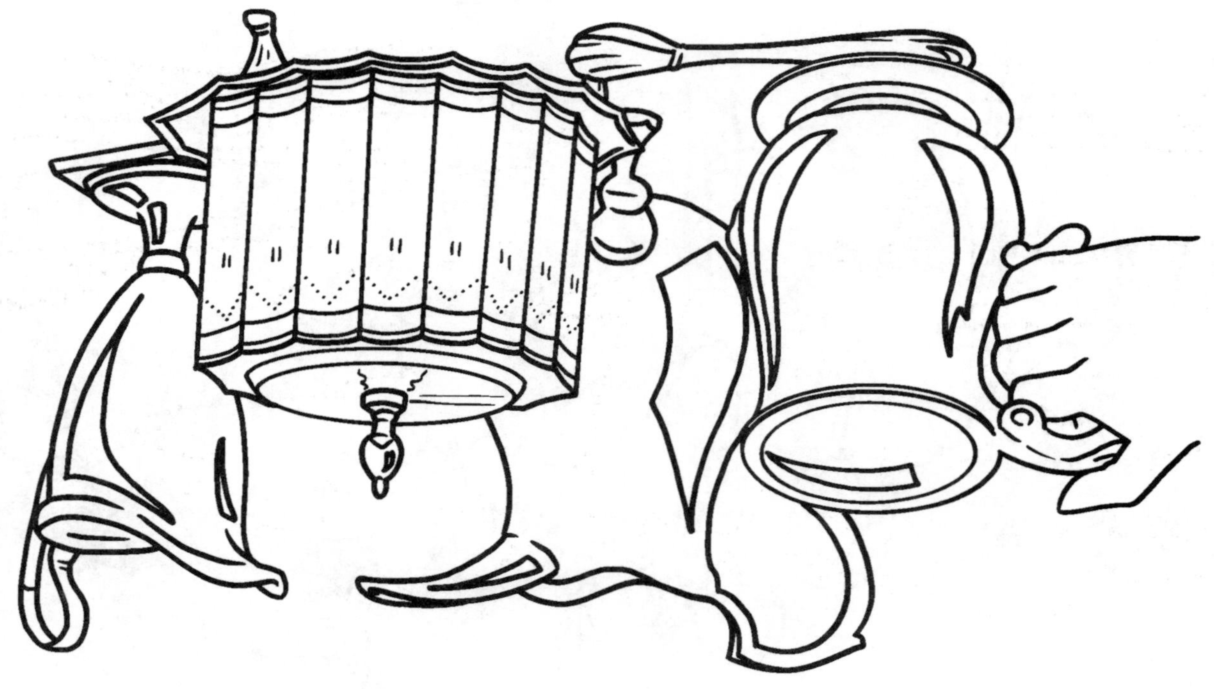

Paul was a silversmith who made teapots.

2

The British put taxes on tea. That made Paul and his friends mad. They took part in the Boston Tea Party. 5

The British soldiers, or "Redcoats," were telling the colonists to do things they did not want to do.

4

The patriots found out that the Redcoats were planning to attack the towns of Lexington and Concord.

7

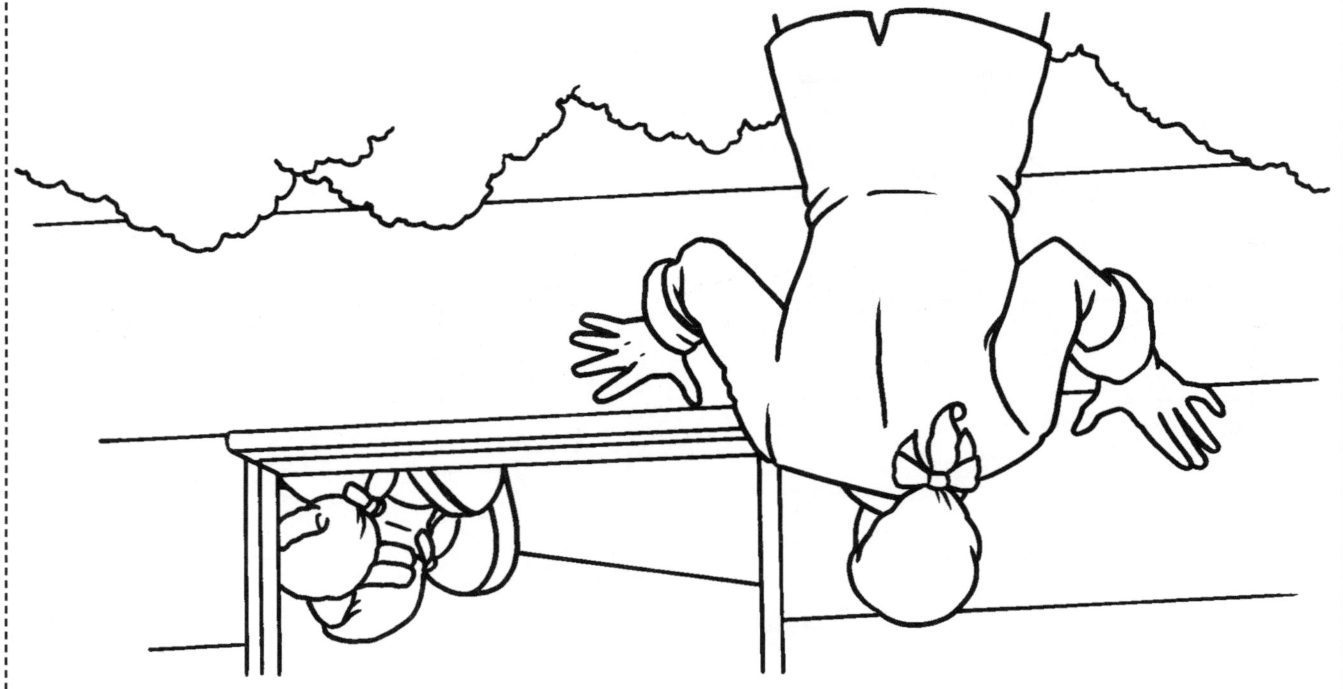

Paul was also a courier who carried important messages for Boston patriots.

6

The next morning, the Revolutionary War began. Paul Revere had arrived in Lexington in time to warn Samual Adams and John Hancock. We are proud of Paul Revere. 9

Paul's helper, Robert Newman, lit two lanterns in a church tower because he saw the British coming in ships. It was an important signal. 8

Paul rode on horseback at midnight. He shouted, "The British are coming" to warn the people that the British were coming. 10

Lewis and Clark

The third president of the United States, Thomas Jefferson, was very interested in the land west of the Mississippi River. He wanted a land route to the Pacific Ocean that would follow the Missouri and Columbia Rivers. These rivers would provide transportation that would assist in the establishment of a fur trade with the Native Americans. In 1803, Congress approved funds for an expedition to explore this land. In the meantime, Jefferson negotiated the purchase of the Louisiana Territory. The Louisiana Purchase nearly doubled the size of the United States. (Later, 13 states would be established on the land.) It included lands stretching from the Mississippi River to the Rocky Mountains and from the Gulf of Mexico to the Canadian border. This land purchase insured that the people in the expedition would be traveling on American territory.

President Jefferson chose Meriwether Lewis, his private secretary, to lead the expedition. Lewis, a neighbor of Thomas Jefferson's, had grown up in Virginia. He was knowledgeable about plants and animals and was an Army captain. Lewis chose his close friend, William Clark, to make the trip with him. Clark was born in Virginia but moved to the frontier of Kentucky. Clark served in the army and fought in the Indian Wars in the Northwest Territory. Both these men were experienced soldiers, had dealt with the Native Americans, and were accustomed to frontier life.

Lewis studied astronomy, botony, and medicine before departing on the expedition. He was responsible for gathering supplies for his men and materials to be used in trade on the journey. Lewis also took charge of the building of the boat that they would need to begin their journey. In December of 1803, William Clark went to St. Louis to begin enlisting men and soldiers to join the expeditions. He sought strong, healthy men with diverse talents. They would need hunters, interpreters, and river experts.

The expedition of 45 people departed on May 14, 1804. After traveling in boats on the Missouri River for five months, the group reached Mandan (now North Dakota) where they would spend the winter. There they met a French-Canadian named Toussaint Charbonneau and his pregnant wife, Sacagawea, who was a member of the Shoshone tribe.

When Sacagawea was 12 years old, she was kidnapped by another Native American tribe. Later, the tribe sold her to Charbonneau and she became his bride. She could speak several Native American languages and knew the land, as well as native foods and herbs. The men realized what an asset her knowledge of the land and language skills would be and invited Sacagawea and her family to travel with them on the expedition. Sacagawea helped serve as a guide and an interpreter to the Native Americans. With her help, the expedition was able to get horses from the Shoshone tribe for the trip across the mountains. When they reached the Columbia River, they again traveled in boats. A year and a half after the expedition began, they reached the Pacific Ocean, at what is now Oregon.

On the trip back, the men separated to explore new lands. They rejoined each other at the Yellowstone and Missouri Rivers. Clark was shocked to learn that Lewis, who wore elkskin clothing, had been mistaken for an elk and had been shot by a hunter. Luckily, he survived. The expedition arrived back home September 23, 1806. The men had explored approximately 8,000 miles of territory. They had valuable records of the trip including maps of their route, drawings of the scenery, and journals documenting the whole trip. Congress rewarded the men by giving them land. Lewis became governor of the Louisiana Territory and Clark became the governor of the Missouri Territory.

Lewis and Clark

Map Study

In 1804, Meriwether Lewis and William Clark began their expedition from St. Louis to the Pacific Ocean.

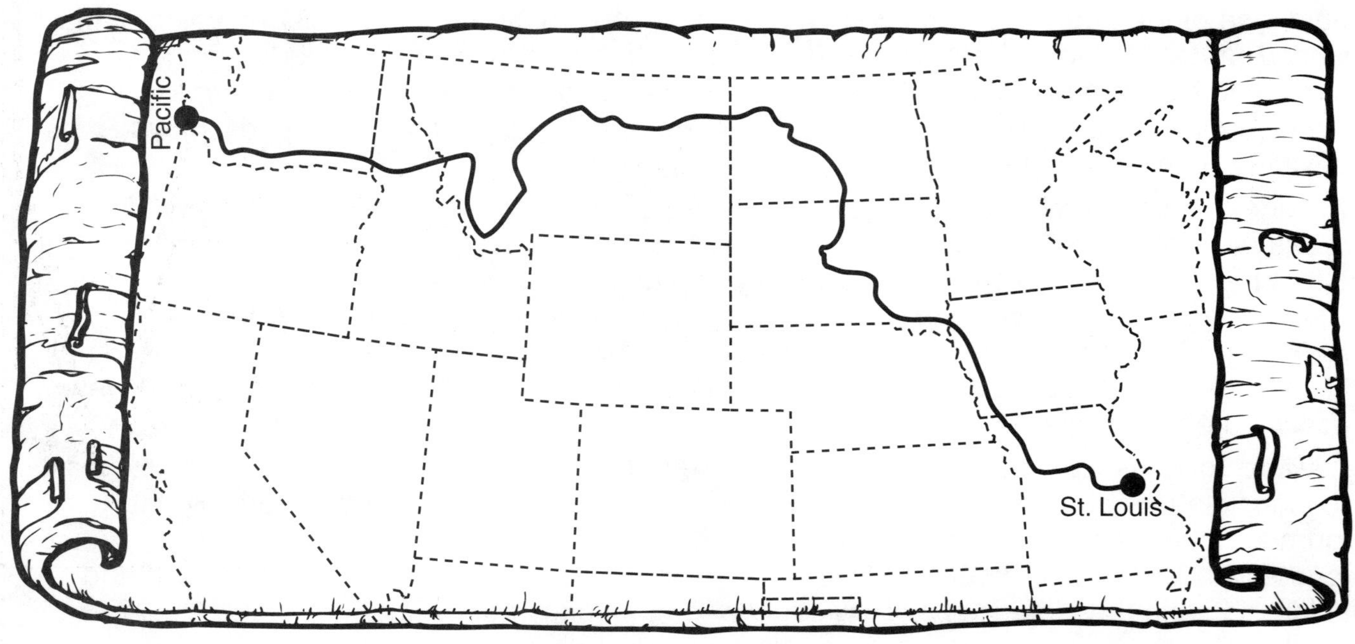

Trace the route followed by Lewis and Clark to and from the Pacific Ocean. Through which states do you pass?

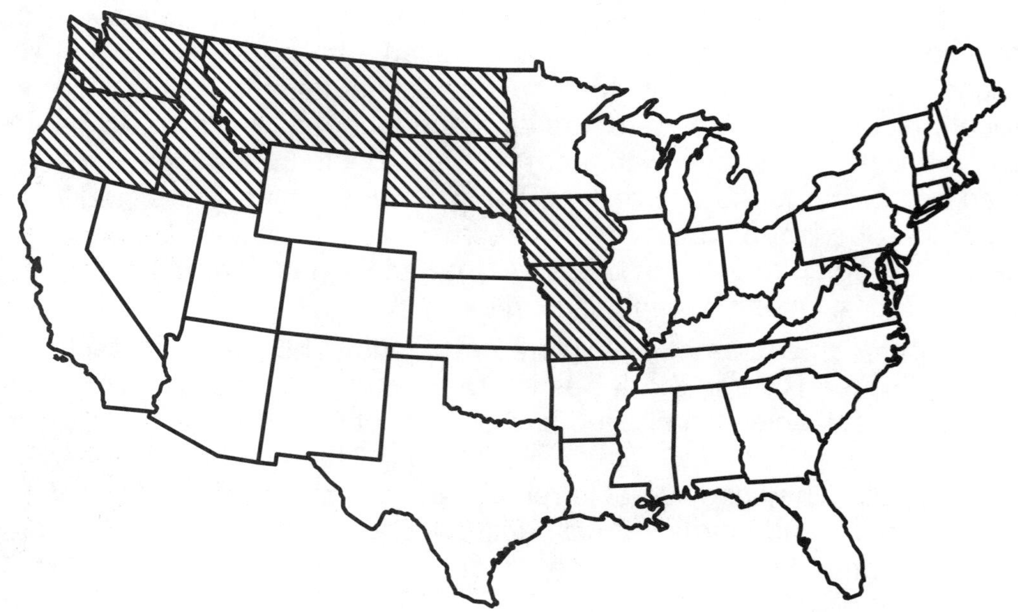

President Thomas Jefferson wanted to find a route to the Pacific Ocean.

1

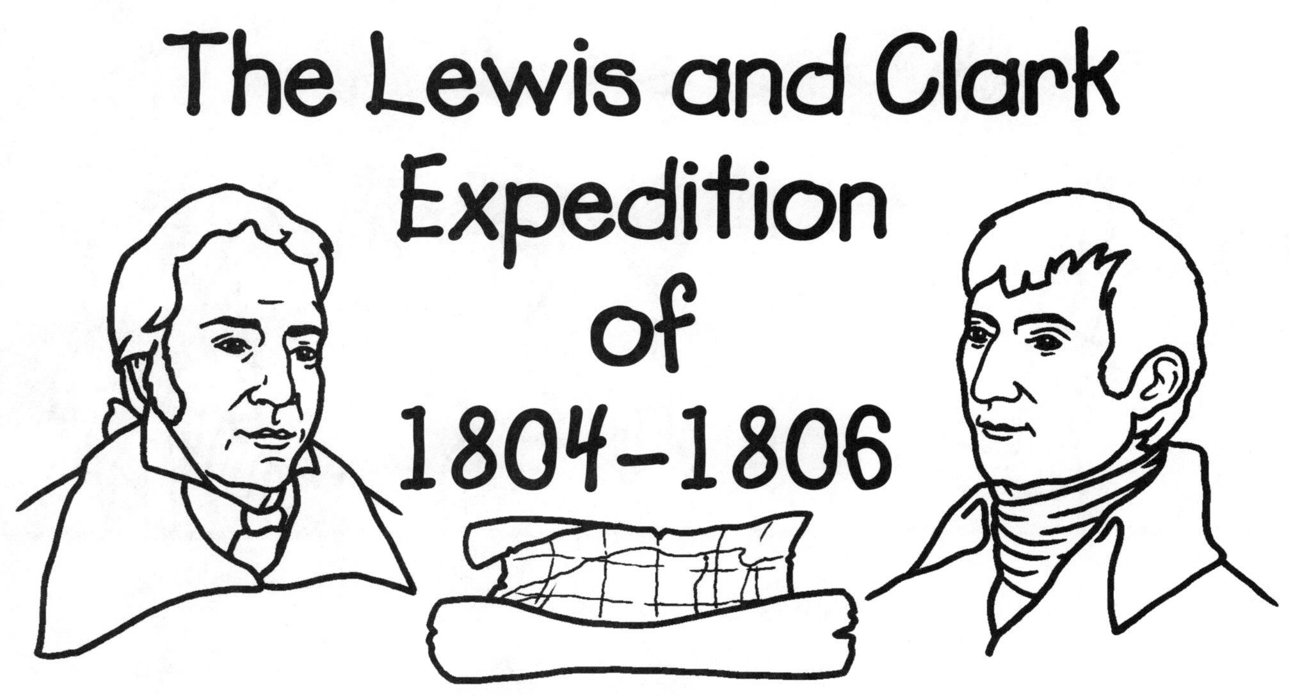

The men asked Sacagawea, a Shoshone woman, to act as their guide and interpreter.

3

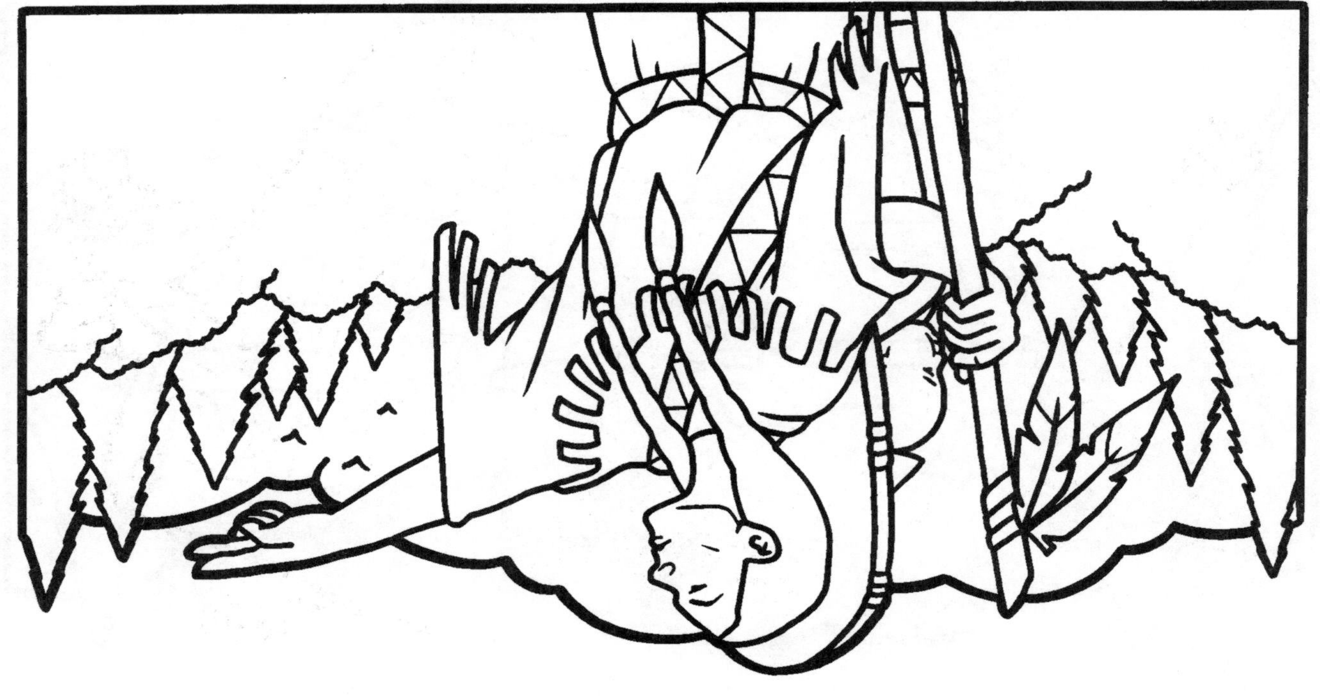

He chose Meriwether Lewis and William Clark to find the way.

2

When they returned home, they had maps, pictures, and journals of the entire trip.

5

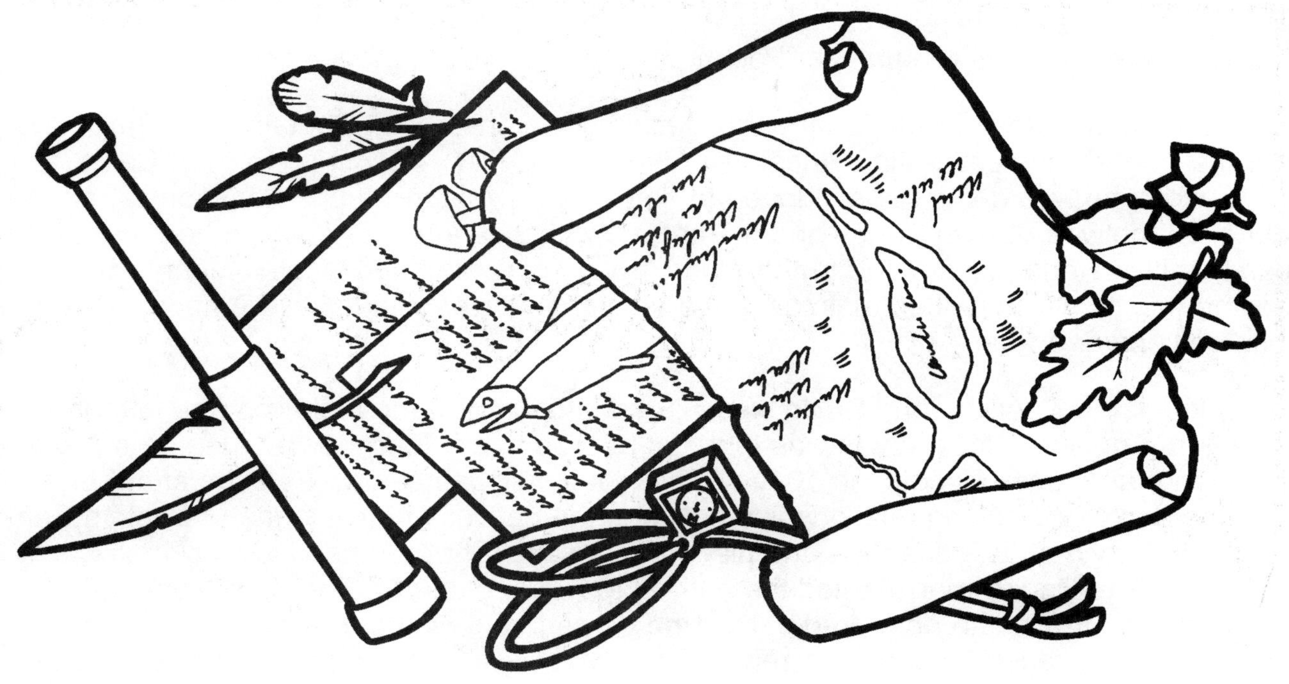

The Lewis and Clark expedition took a year and a half to reach the Pacific Ocean.

4

Pocahontas

Pocahontas was the Native American daughter of Chief Powhatan who was the leader of the Algonquian tribe near the shores of Virginia. She was born in the late 1500s and named Matoaka. Matoaka was nicknamed "Pocahontas" which means *playful one*.

The most famous story about Pocahontas details when she saved Captain John Smith's life after the English had settled in Jamestown, Virginia, in 1607. According to what Captain Smith wrote, he was going to be clubbed to death by Powhatan's men. Pocahontas ran in and put herself between Smith's body and the natives with weapons. She asked her father to spare his life. Regardless of the truth to the story, Pocahontas and Captain John Smith became friends which helped maintain good relations between the Native Americans and the white settlers for awhile.

Some time later, Captain John Smith was injured in a gunpowder explosion and left Virginia to go back to England. Pocahontas was told that he was dead. Pocahontas married a Native American man named Kocoum in 1610. She did not visit Jamestown as often after her marriage due to worsening relationships between the natives and white man. Captain Samuel Argall had Pocahontas kidnapped and placed on a ship. She was used to blackmail Chief Powhatan. The Englishmen wanted the natives to return captured English prisoners, food, and weapons. Powhatan answered part of the demand but did not return everything as requested. As a result, Pocahontas remained in captivity. At first, she was unhappy. Later, she adjusted to her new life and began to convert to Christianity. She moved to a different settlement led by Sir Thomas Dale and there she met and fell in love with John Rolfe. John Rolfe and Pocahontas were married in 1614 and the fighting between the English and the Native Americans diminished.

Pocahontas was baptized and her name became Rebecca. In 1616, the Rolfe family, which included baby Thomas Rolfe, sailed to London with Sir Thomas Dale who wanted money to help the settlement in Virginia. Dale took several Native Americans on the voyage but the biggest sensation was Pocahontas. She was treated like royalty. She met the king and other important people in London. She also reunited with Captain John Smith whom she thought was dead.

In 1617, the Rolfe family started sailing back to Virginia. Pocahontas became so ill that they took her back to England. She died at the age of 22 (approximately) and was buried in Gravesend, England.

Young Thomas Rolfe, Pocahontas' son, was educated in England but later returned to America and served an important role in the history of Virginia. Pocahontas played a significant role in our history. She helped bridge the gap between the Native Americans and the Englishmen.

Pocahontas

Map Study

Pocahontas helped the settlers who established Jamestown in the early 1600s.

Pocahontas was the Native American daughter of Chief Powhatan.

1

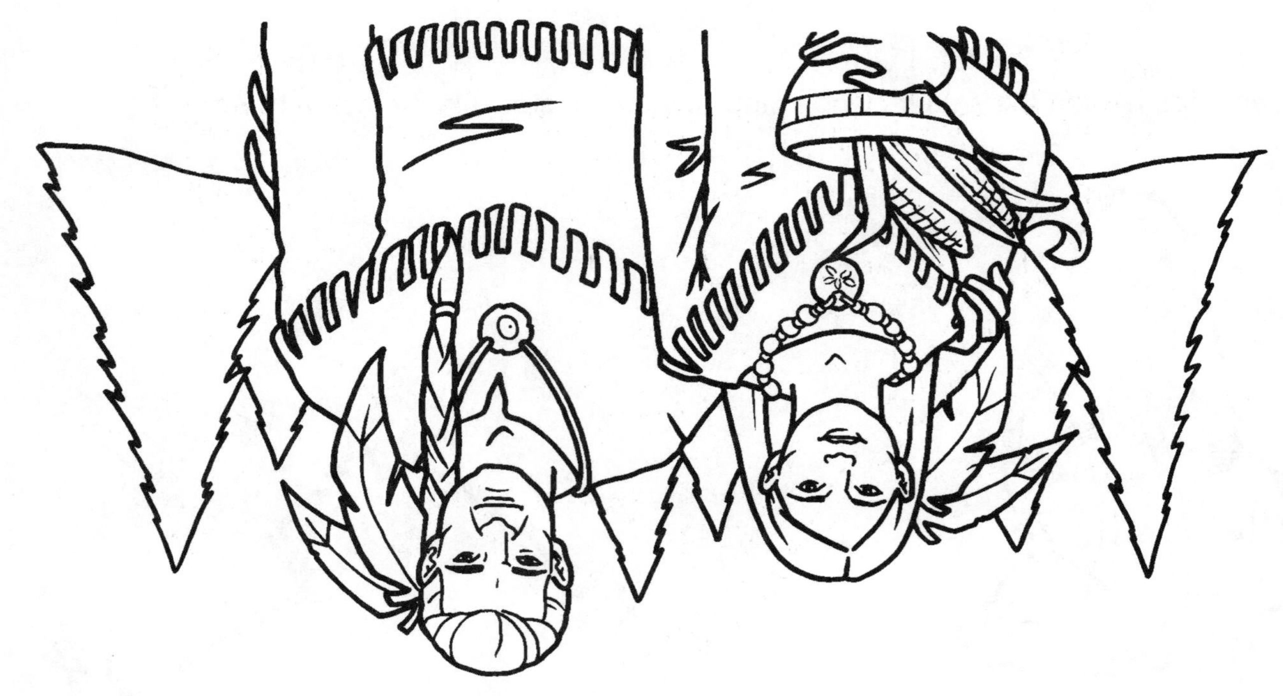

Pocahontas

Circa 1595–1617

At that time, Englishmen had sailed to this area. They called the settlement Jamestown. Pocahontas brought them food.

3

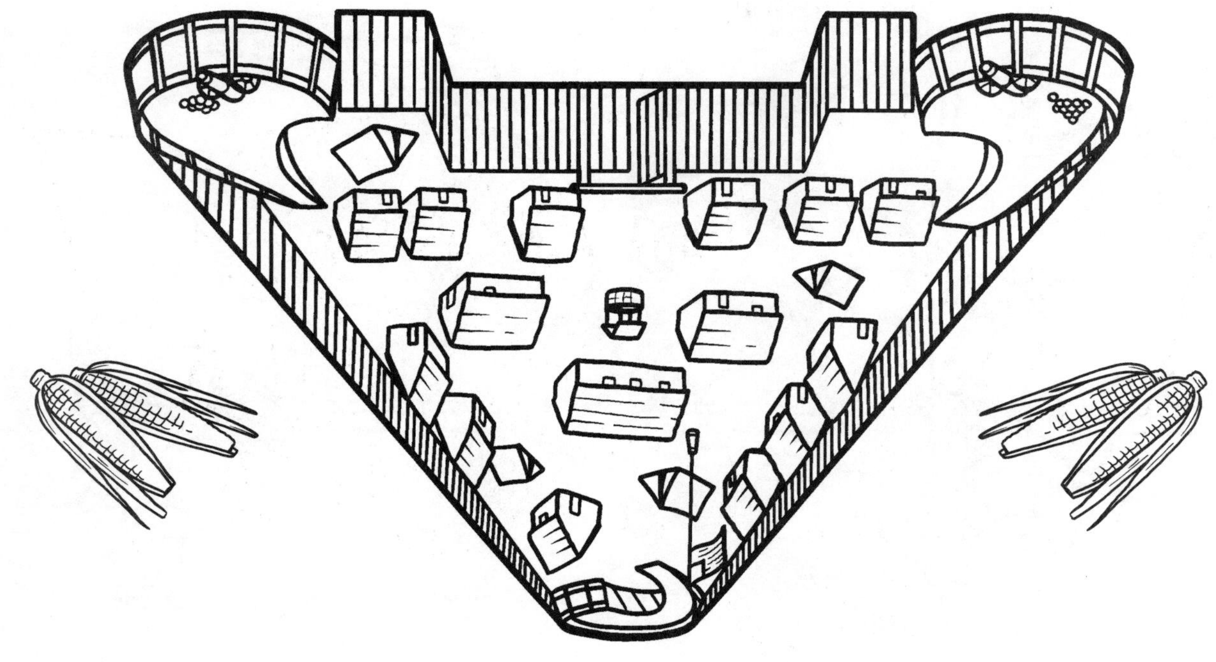

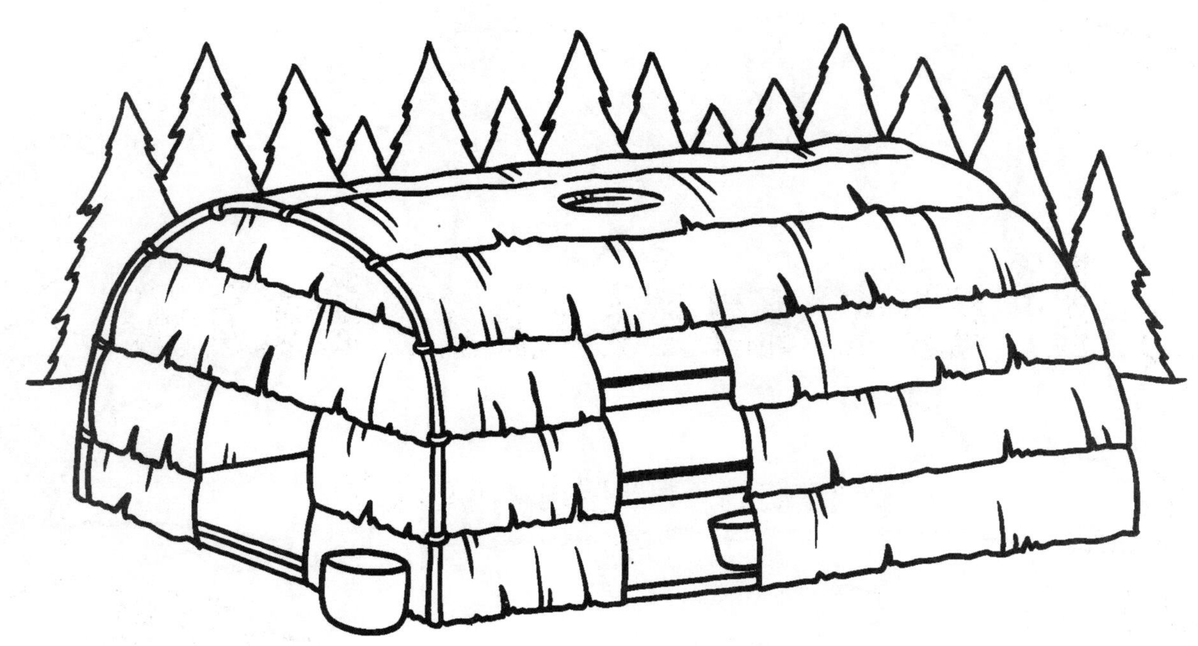

They lived on the land in what is now Virginia.

2

Later, during the struggle between natives and white settlers, Pocahontas was captured.

5

Legend says that Chief Powhatan planned to kill Captain John Smith, a Jamestown settler, but Pocahontas saved his life.

4

Together, they traveled back to England. She met with the king of England.

7

While in captivity, she met and fell in love with John Rolfe.

6

Pocahontas died before she could return to America. She had worked hard to bring peace between the Native Americans and the white settlers.

8

Putting Together Pop-up Books

Materials

For each student you will need:

- copies of text and illustrations
- markers or crayons
- scissors
- glue
- 9" x 12" construction paper for cover

Assembly Directions

1. Color the illustrations. 	2. Cut out the illustrations. 
3. Fold a piece of construction paper in half to serve as the front and back covers of the book. 	4. Cut out and glue the cover page to the center-front of the book cover. 
5. Fold each interior page in half on the solid line. The top of the page should be folded to the back so that the dashed lines are visible for cutting. 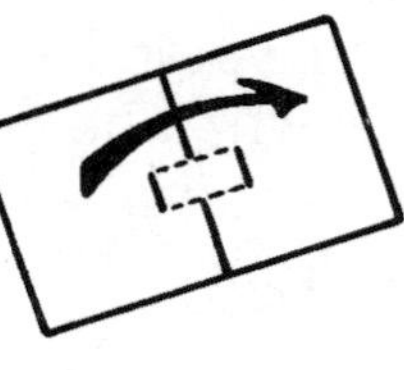	6. Cut along the dashed lines, being sure to cut through both layers of the folded paper. Cut all the way to the large dots. 
7. Open the page and fold it back the other way, holding the cut section between your fingers, keeping it folded. Close the page, flattening the cut part so that when you re-open the page, it will be "popped up." 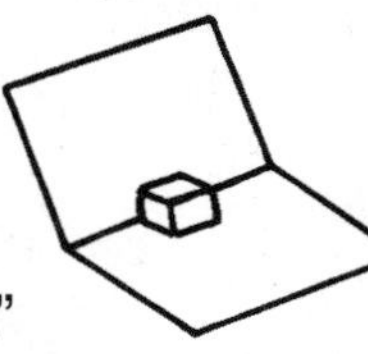	8. Spread glue over gray box and attach the illustration. **Note:** In order to ensure that the illustration does not bend when the book closes, glue it so it extends beyond the pop-up. 
9. Arrange the pages in numerical order. Glue the back of one page to the front of the other until all are together as a booklet. 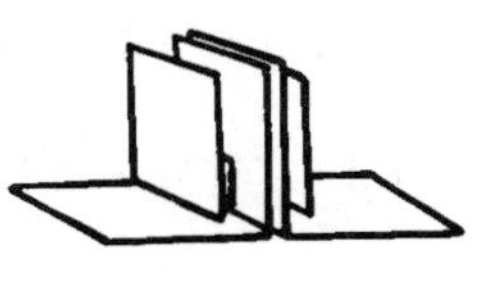	10. Glue the booklet to the inside of the cover. 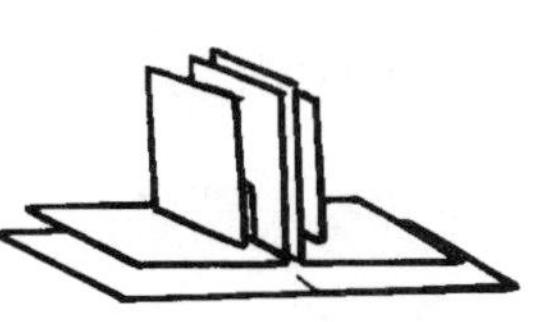

Johnny Appleseed

John Chapman, later given the name Johnny Appleseed, was born in Leominster, Massachusetts, on September 26, 1774. John's father was a Minuteman who later fought in the Revolutionary War. John's mother died when he was very young.

John became a legendary figure when he left home and began traveling the Ohio Valley area (Ohio and Indiana) in the 1800s. People picture him as being a big and strong man, but John Chapman was actually small in stature. He lived a very simple life. He preferred walking barefoot, wearing sacks for clothes, and a tin pot for a hat. One thinks of Johnny Appleseed as being very poor but, actually, he owned a lot of land. Of course, he had his land full of apple orchards. He planted his first orchard in 1796 in western Pennsylvania.

As he traveled through Ohio, Pennsylvania, Kentucky, Indiana, and Illinois, he would give pioneers deerskin bags full of apple seeds that he collected from cider mills in Pennsylvania. People would pay him for the seeds with money but mostly with goods such as used clothing. He would later go back to the areas where the seeds had been planted and help tend the orchards. The orchards were an asset to the economy of the Ohio Valley. Apples were also an excellent source of food for the diets of the early settlers.

Not only would John give people seeds and seedlings, but he also would tell stories about his many traveling adventures and talk about his faith. John Chapman was a deeply religious man. His church was based on the teachings of Emanuel Swedeborg from Sweden. Swedenborgians were very rare in the country.

Many legendary tales are told about Johnny Appleseed. He slept outdoors and it was said when he couldn't find water, he would melt snow with his feet. It also was said that when he was in Kentucky, John met a tall, thin young man named Abe Lincoln headed back home after borrowing a book from someone. He gave him a bag of seeds.

John Chapman roamed the forests without any gun. He was a friend to the wild animals and a spiritual man to the settlers. The Native Americans thought of him as a medicine man because he would give herbs and plants used for healing. John Chapman was a hero and a welcome visitor to the frontier people.

He died on March 18, 1845, from pneumonia at the home of good friend, William Worth. He was buried in Ft. Wayne, Indiana, under a tombstone that reads, "He lived for others."

Johnny Appleseed

Map Study

Johnny Appleseed traveled from his home in Massachusetts throughout the Ohio Valley region.

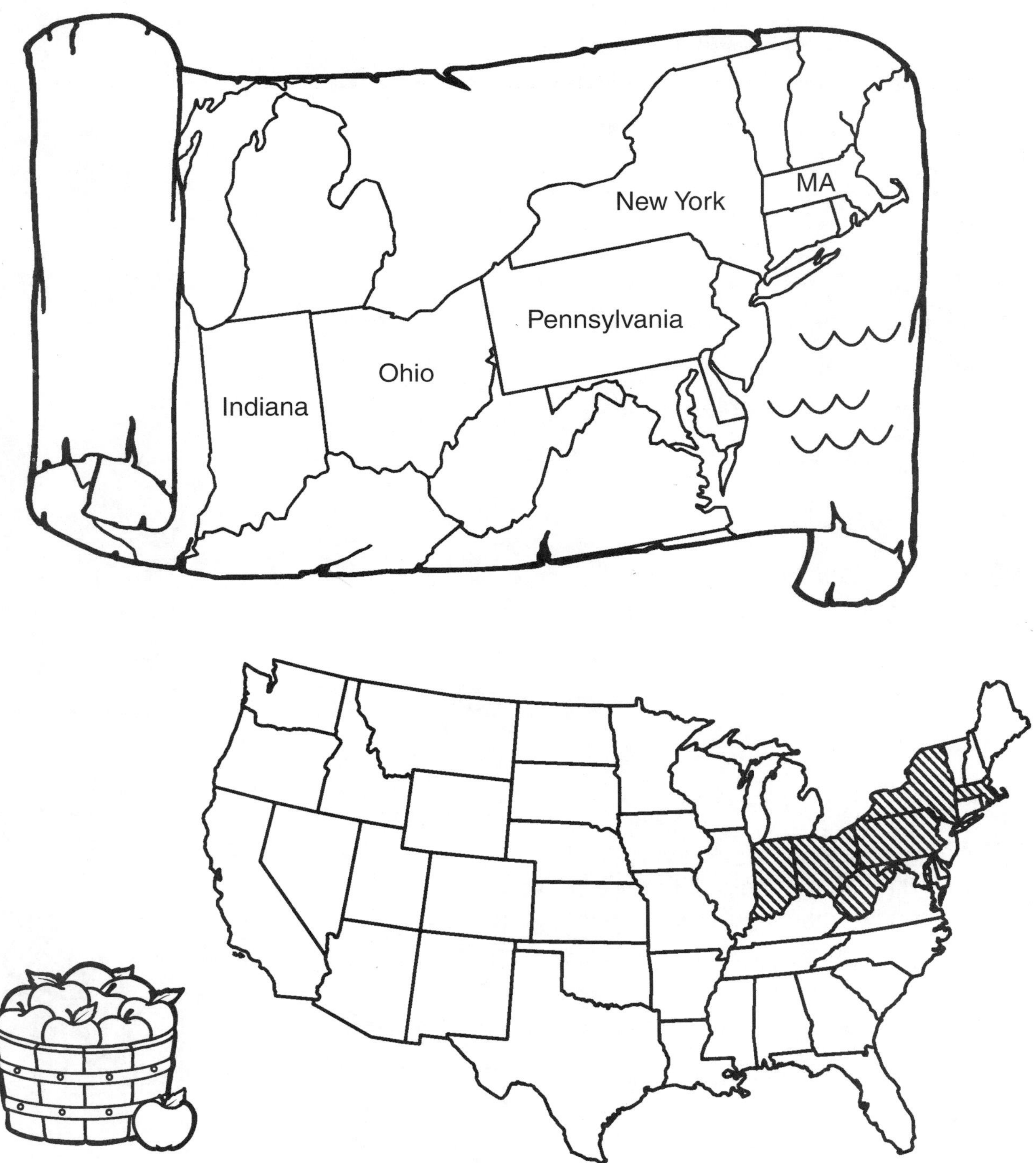

Putting Together *Johnny Appleseed*

Materials

- copies of the illustrations (pages 52 and 53)
- copies of the text pages (pages 43–51)
- crayons, colored pencils, or markers
- red, black, or green construction paper
- scissors
- glue

Assembly Directions for the *Johnny Appleseed* Pop-up Book

1. Follow the general directions for pop-up books on page 39.
2. Order the pages as follows:

   Page 1—Johnny Appleseed

   Page 2—apple

   Page 3—spade

   Page 4—seeds

   Page 5—apple tree

   Page 6—orchard

   Page 7—pot

   Page 8—Johnny and pot

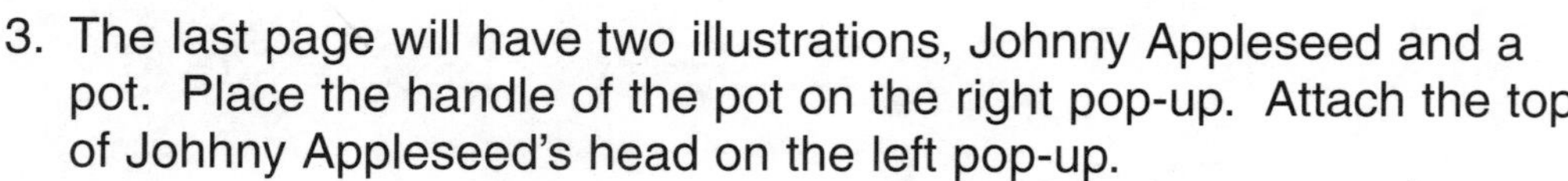

3. The last page will have two illustrations, Johnny Appleseed and a pot. Place the handle of the pot on the right pop-up. Attach the top of Johnny Appleseed's head on the left pop-up.

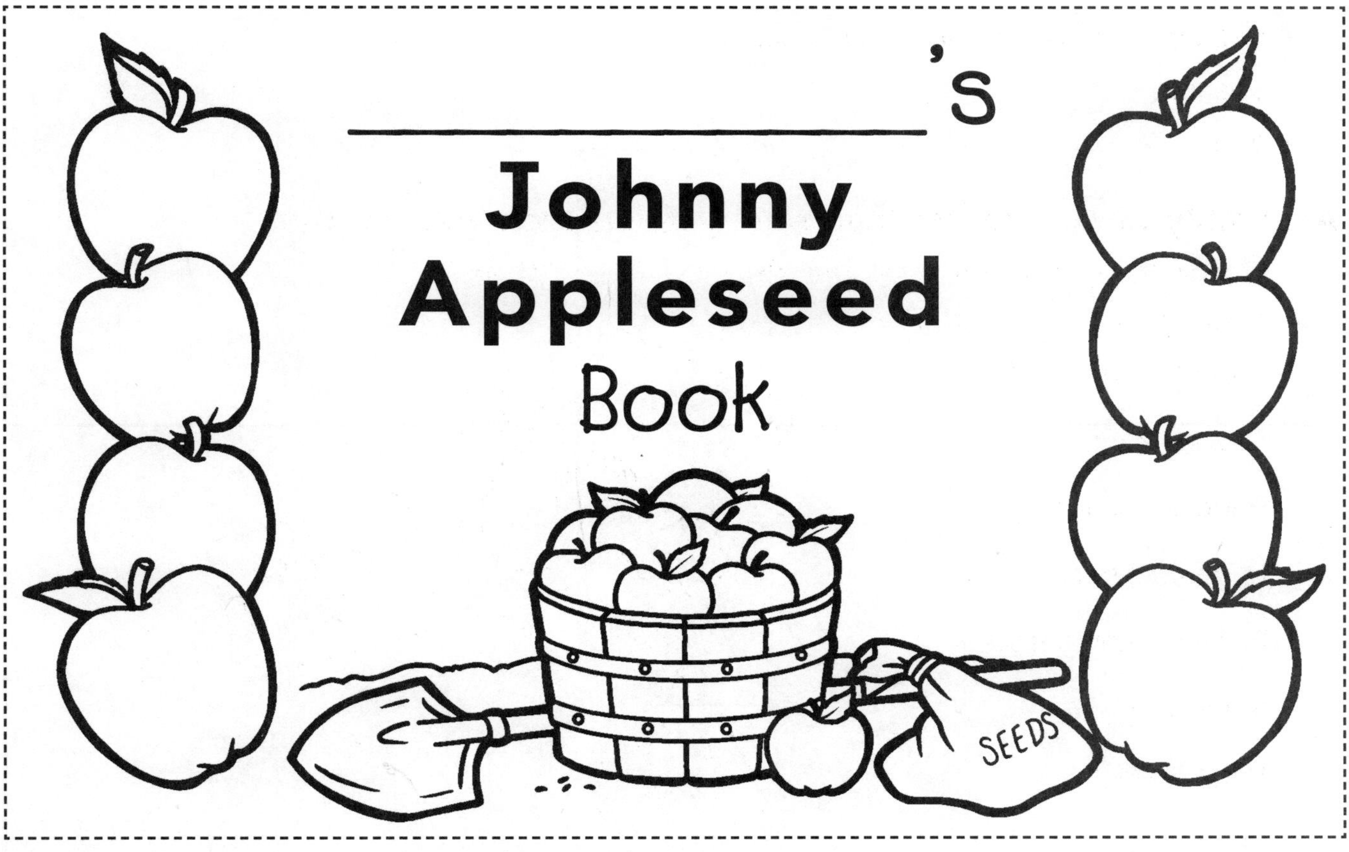

cover

John Chapman

Glue

Johnny Appleseed

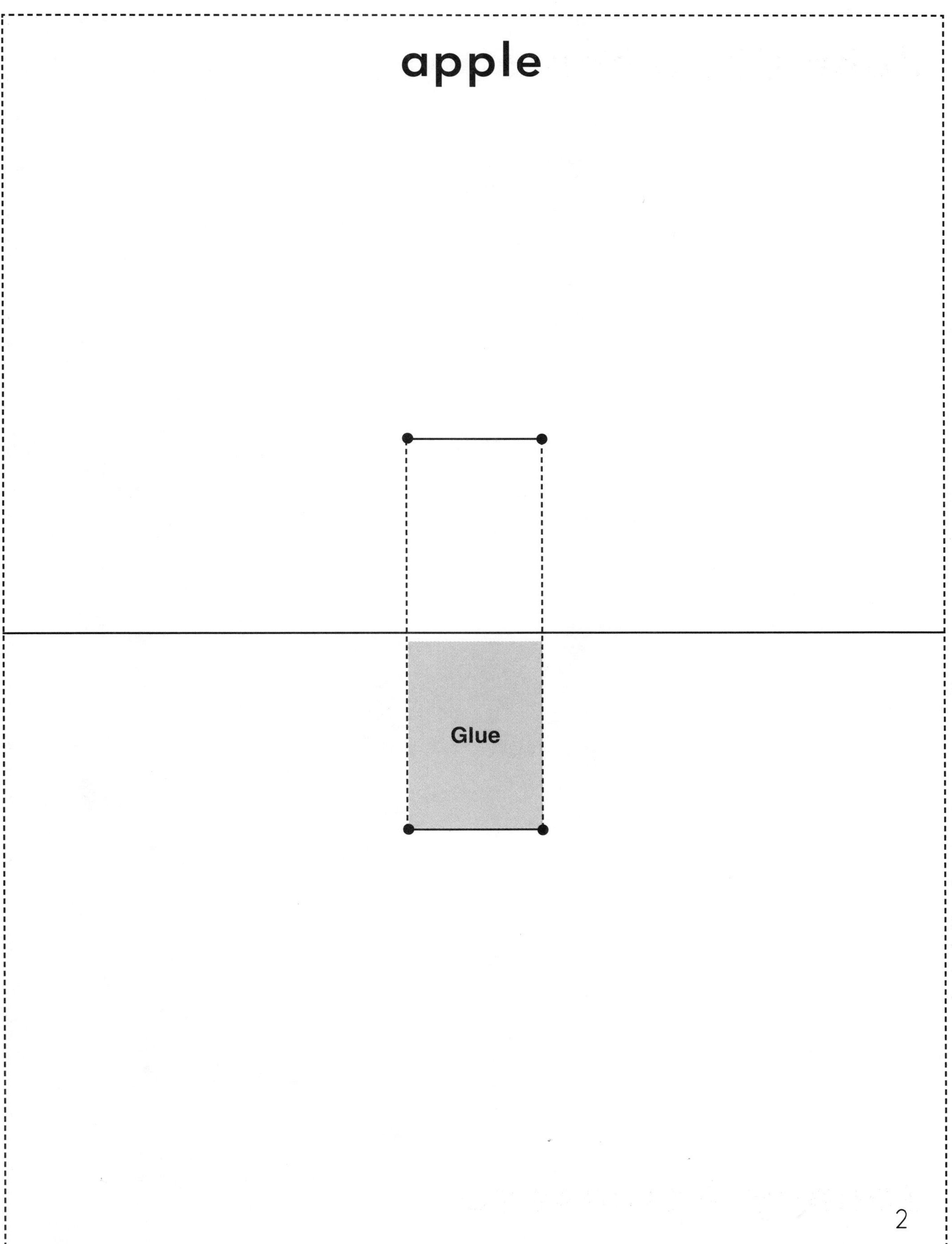
apple
Glue
2

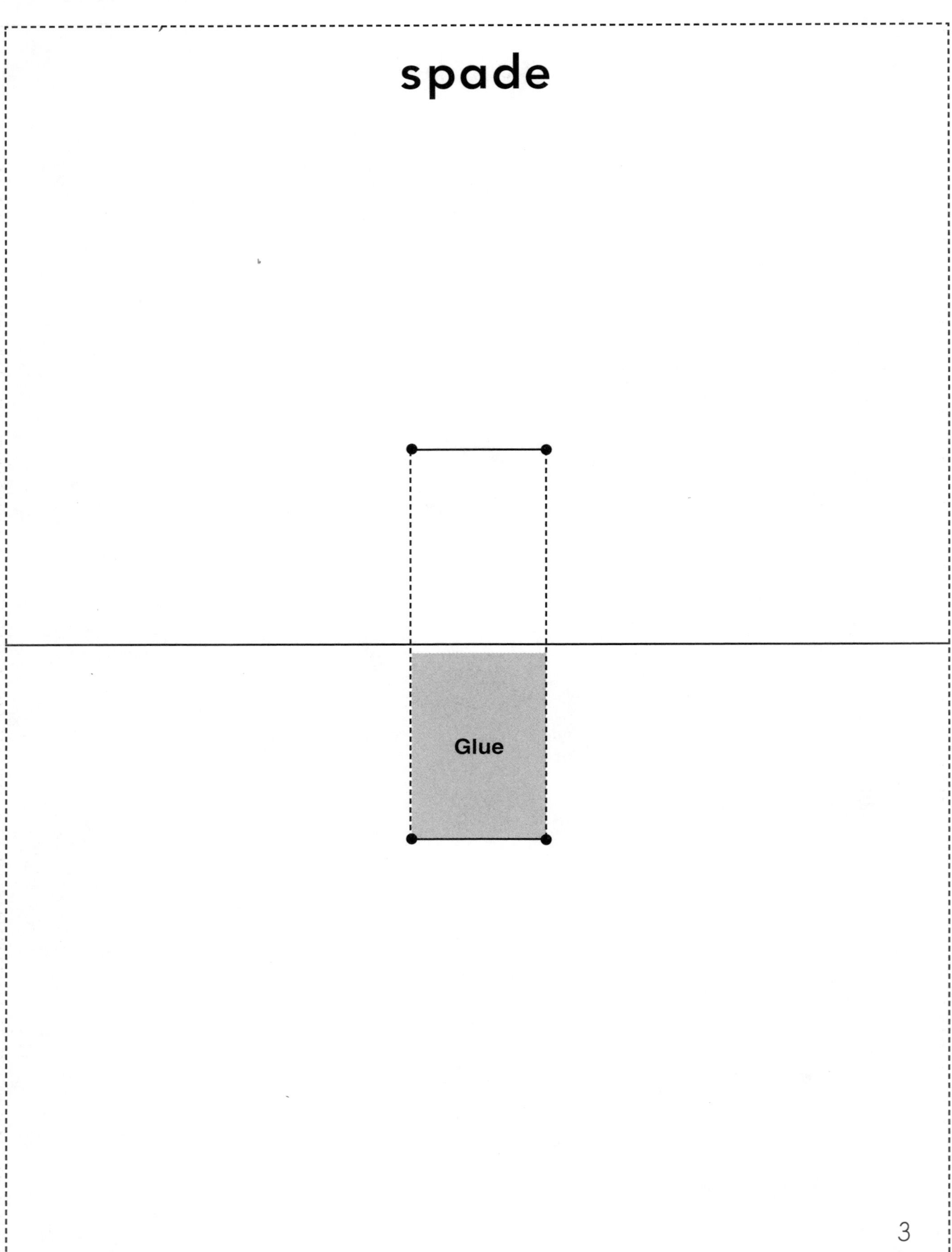
spade
Glue
3

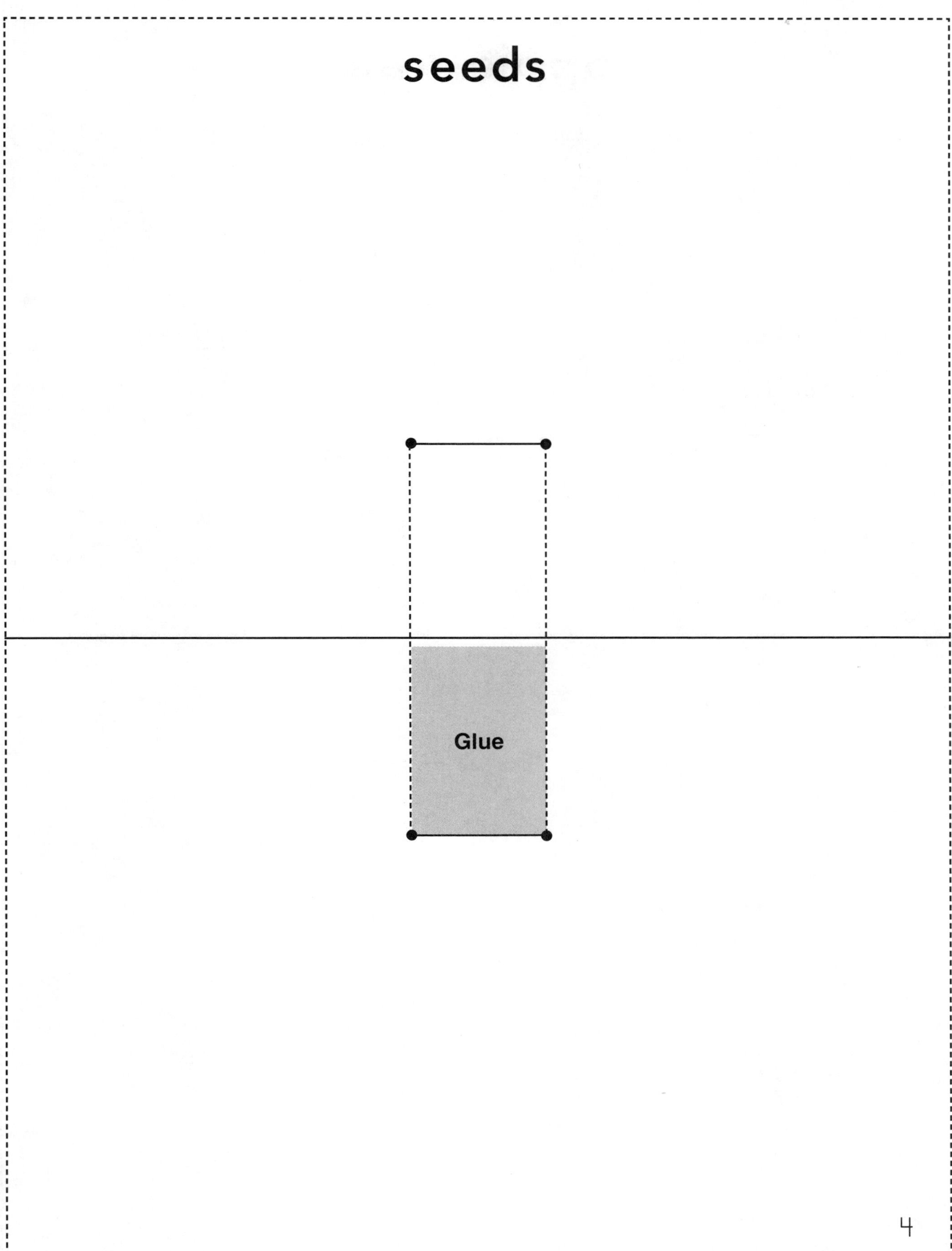
seeds
Glue
4

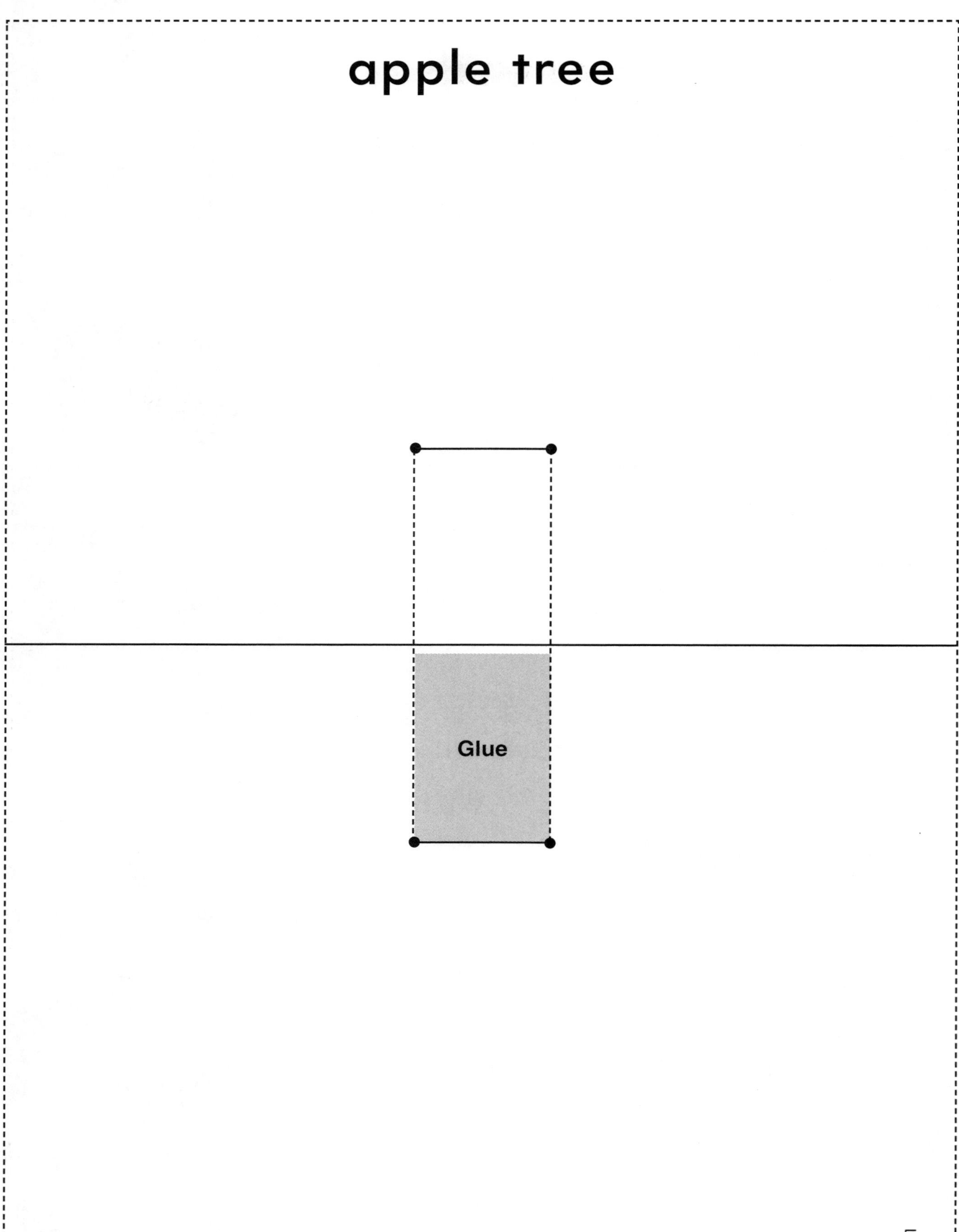
apple tree
Glue
5

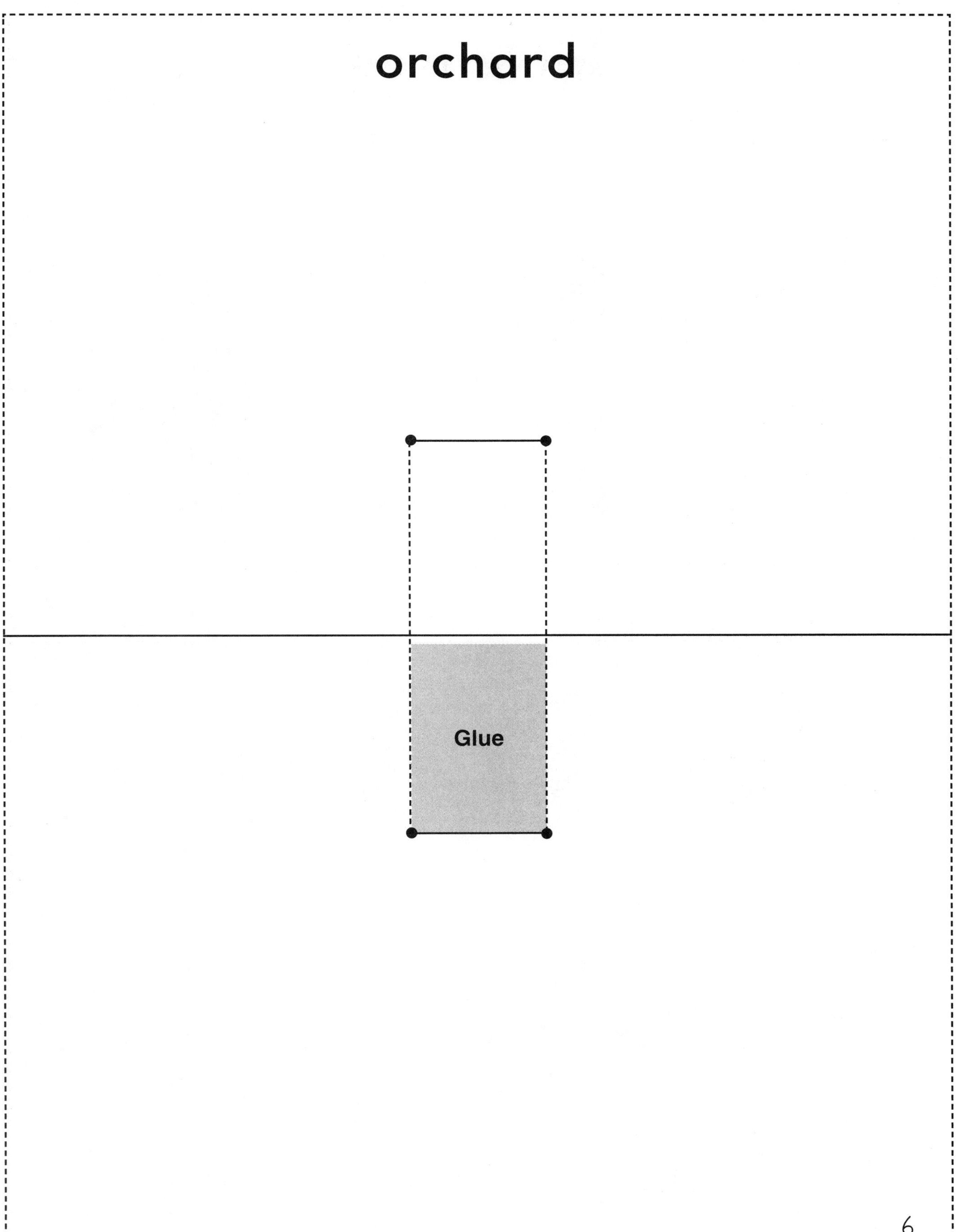
orchard
Glue
6

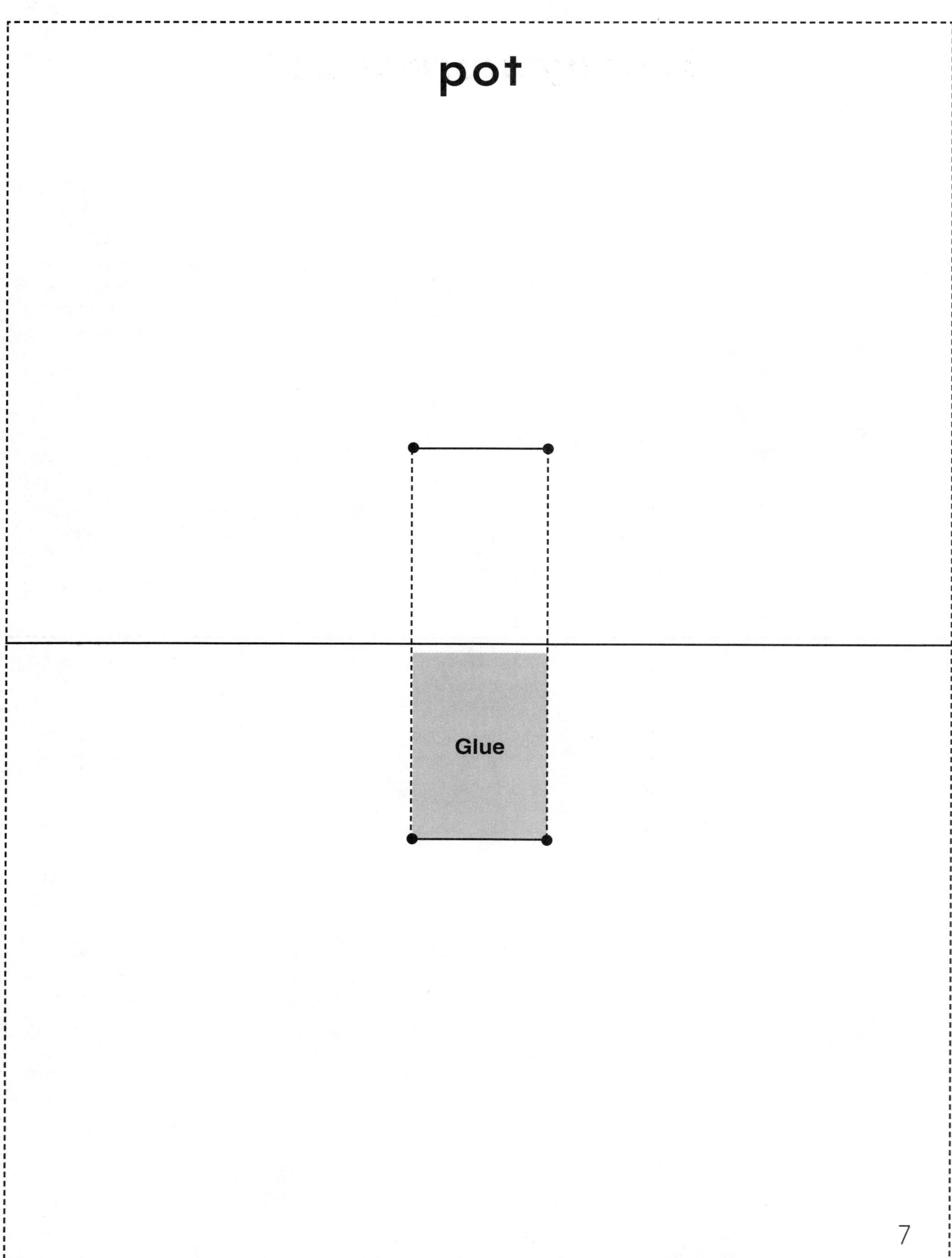
pot
Glue
7

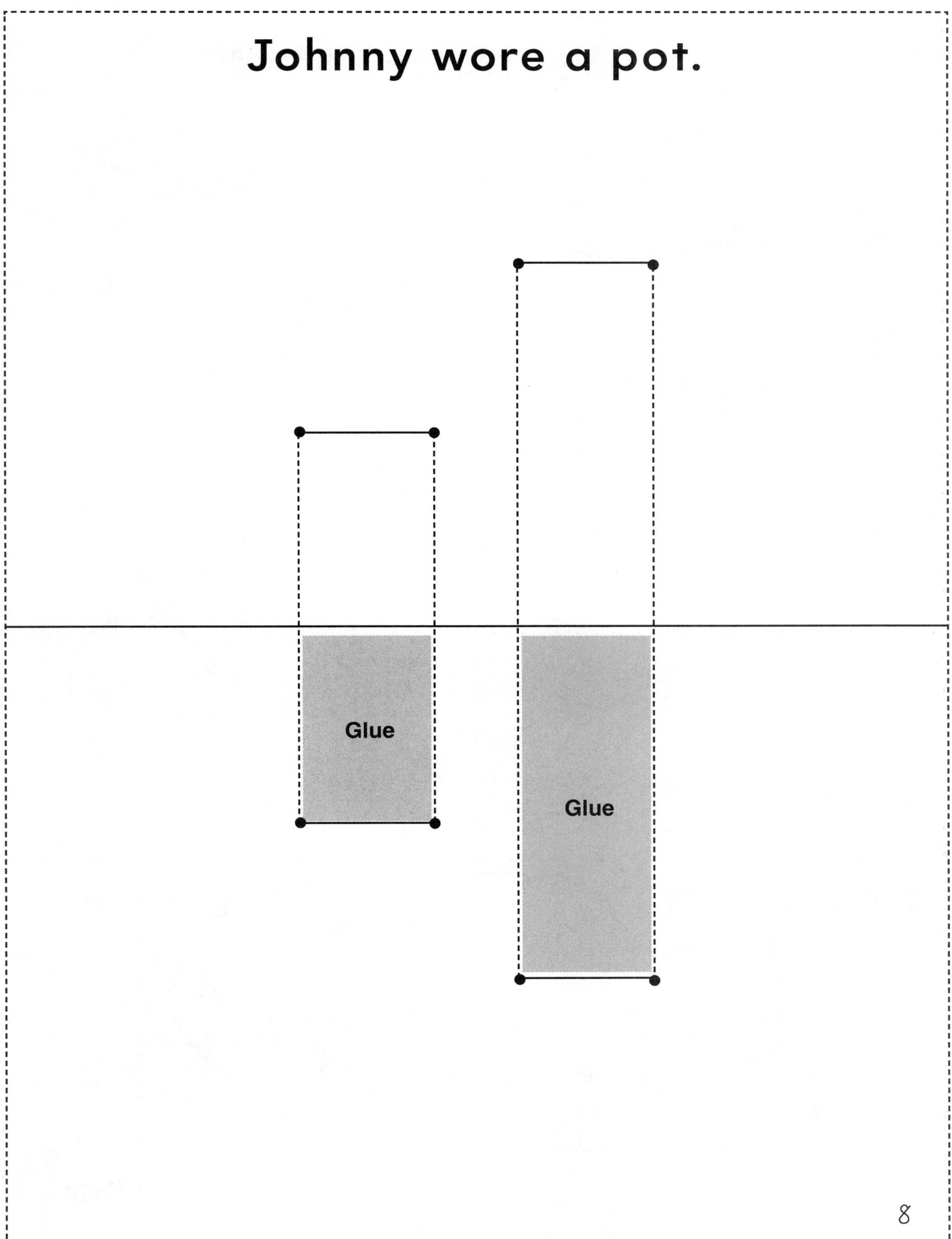
Johnny wore a pot.
Glue
Glue
8

Page 1

Page 2

Page 3

Page 4

Page 6

Johnny Appleseed

Page 5

Page 7

Page 8

Page 8

Booker T. Washington

Booker T. Washington was born on April 5, 1856, in rural Virginia. For the first nine years of his life, he was owned as a slave. When freed, he moved with his family to West Virginia where they worked in the salt and coal mines. At age 16, he attended what is now Hampton University in Virginia. At the time, it was a new college for African-American people called Hampton Normal and Agricultural Institute. He graduated in 1875 and began teaching.

Booker taught school and attended Wayland Seminary before returning to Hampton to teach at the Hampton Institute. He believed in teaching useful skills that could be used to improve one's economic condition. He was assigned to do industrial training for 75 Native Americans. His program was a success. He was asked to start another college in Tuskegee, Alabama, to train black students. He started the school in an abandoned shack donated by a church. There, students learned academics as well as industrial training. They also were responsible for providing the labor required to complete the campus structures. They built classrooms, dorms, and other necessary buildings. Some students were trained to be teachers while others learned trade-related skills.

At that time, Booker T. Washington believed that black people should recognize that they were still secondary citizens. He felt they should learn skills and trades that would be useful in helping them make a place for themselves in the society. His focus was on economic opportunities for his students, rather than civil rights. He knew skilled labor was needed everywhere and he did not want his people to be ashamed of knowing a skill. He felt it would be the key to their advancement.

Booker T. Washington was supported for this thinking by many blacks and whites. Others felt he should be more political and fight for rights, not skills. He was met with opposition from African Americans who refused to be treated as or considered secondary citizens.

He was a spokesperson for black people and an advisor to President Theodore Roosevelt. Before his death in 1915, he had authored several books and founded several organizations. He is remembered for his love of education and his respect for hard work. He was inspirational to many.

Assembly Directions for the *Booker T. Washington* Pop-up Book

1. Follow the general directions for pop-up book assembly on page 39.
2. Place the pictures on the pages in the following order: Booker T. Washington, log cabin, coal mine, Booker with a book, motto, orator.

Optional: Use the pretzels as logs on the cabin and aluminum foil as the roof.

Booker T. Washington

Map Study

Booker T. Washington was born in Franklin County, Virginia. He started the Tuskegee Institute in Alabama in 1881.

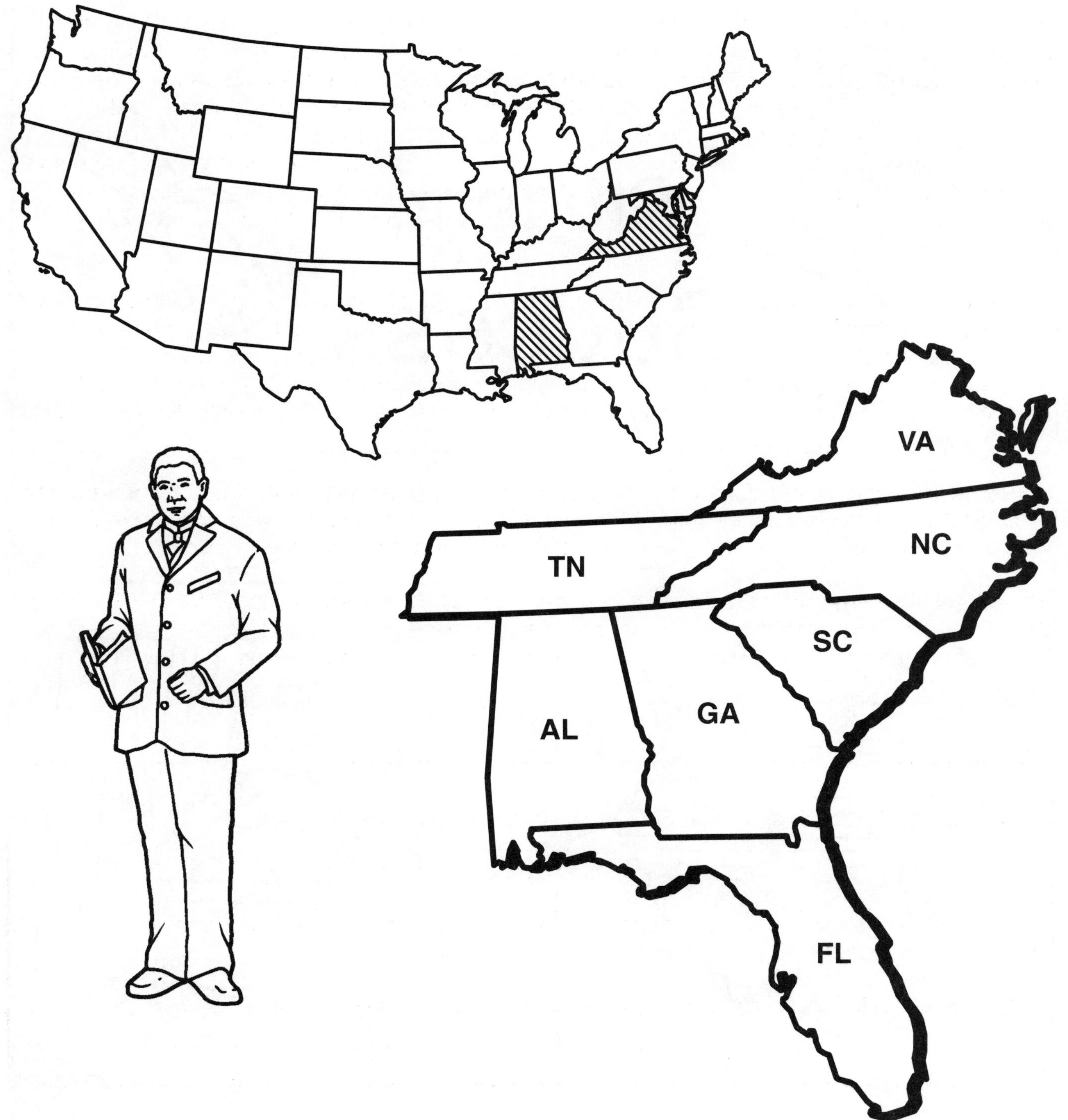

Booker T. Washington

Slave,

Student,

Success

cover

page 1 **page 2**

Glue

In 1856, Booker T. Washington was born in a log cabin in Virginia as a slave.

1

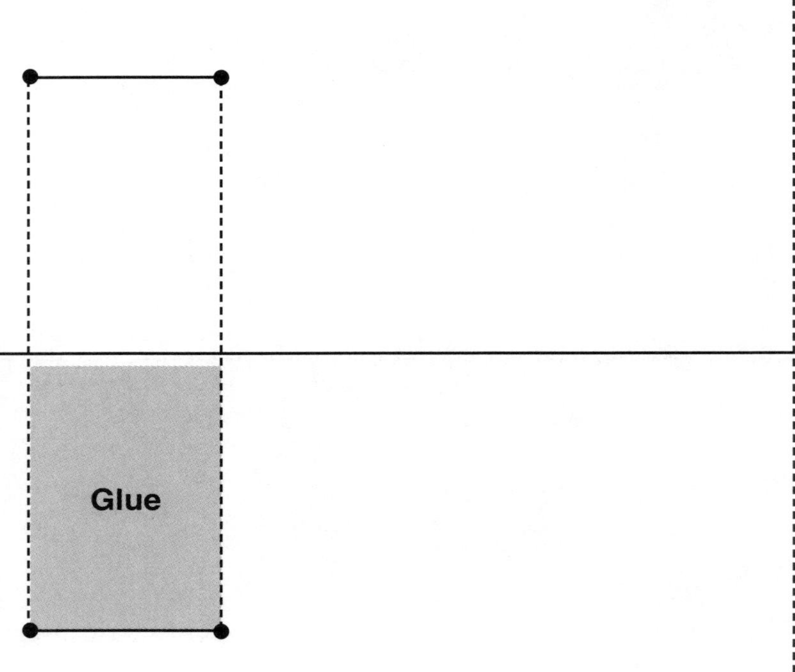

In 1865, when he was nine years old he was freed. He worked in the salt mines in West Virginia.

2

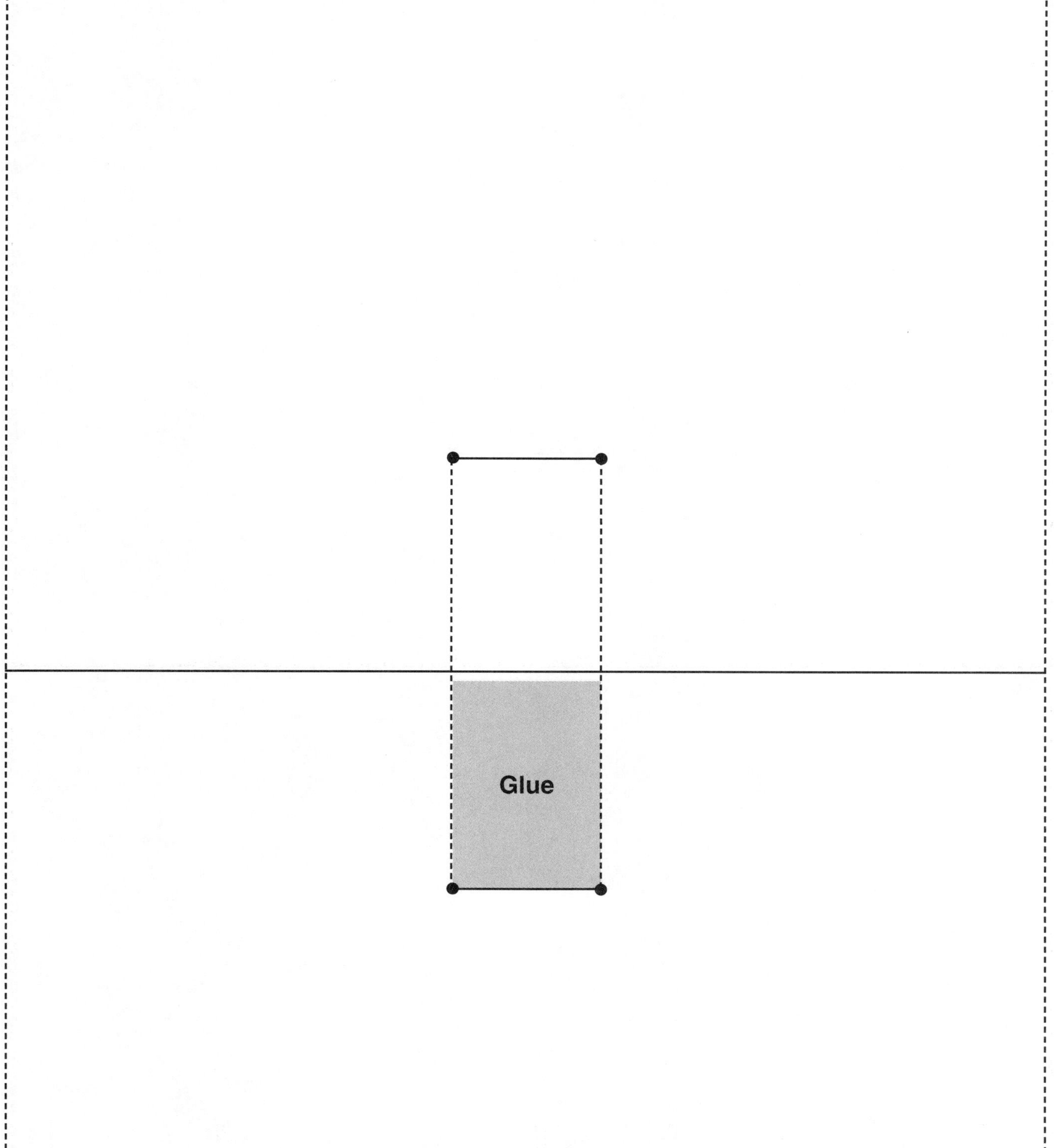

Young Booker really wanted to learn to read. Somehow, his mother got a book for him. Booker taught himself to read.

3

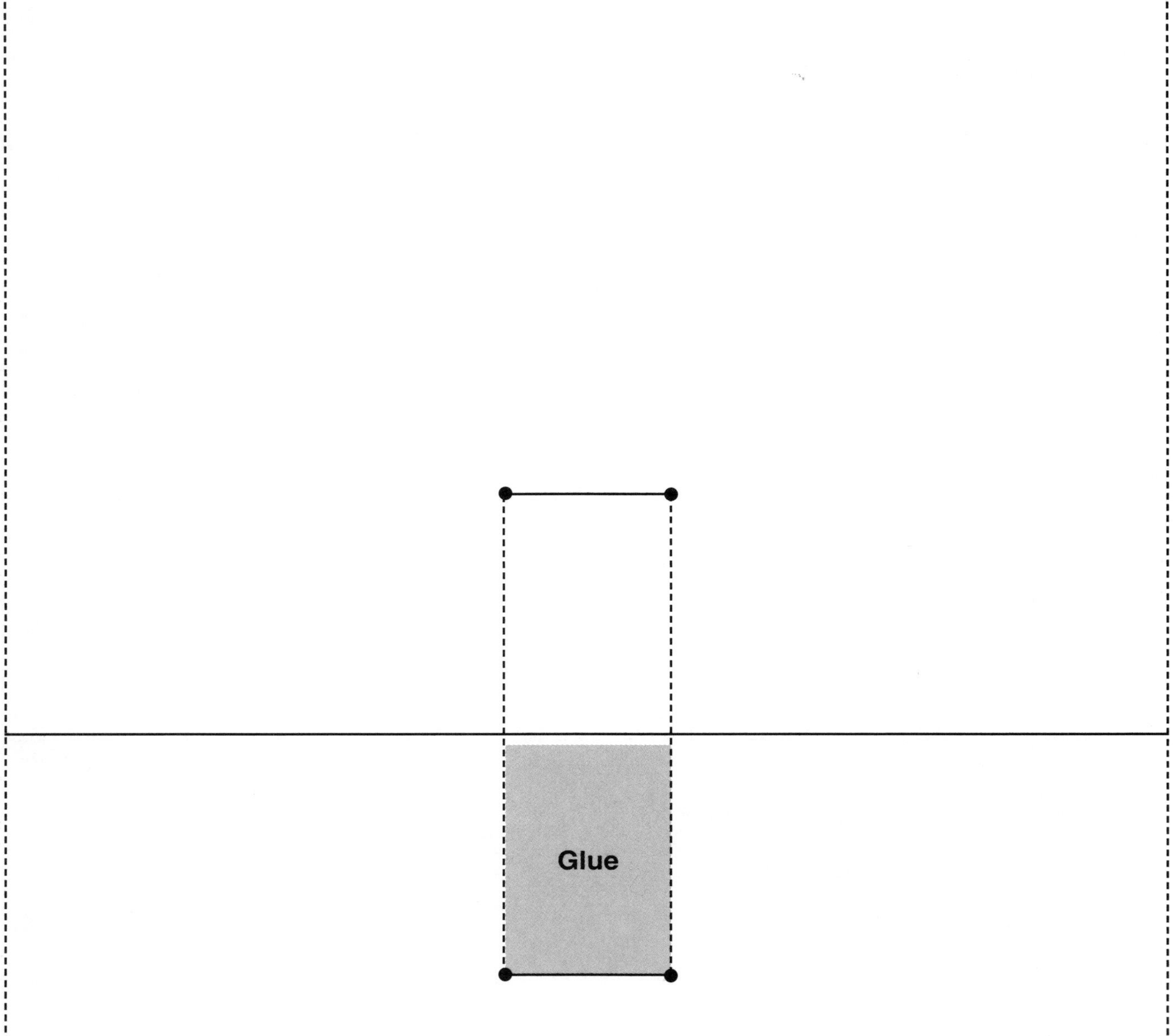

Booker set high goals for himself. After he graduated, he started a college for African Americans called the Tuskegee Institute. Every student who attended helped build it. Their motto was "In Industry the Foundation Must be Laid."

4

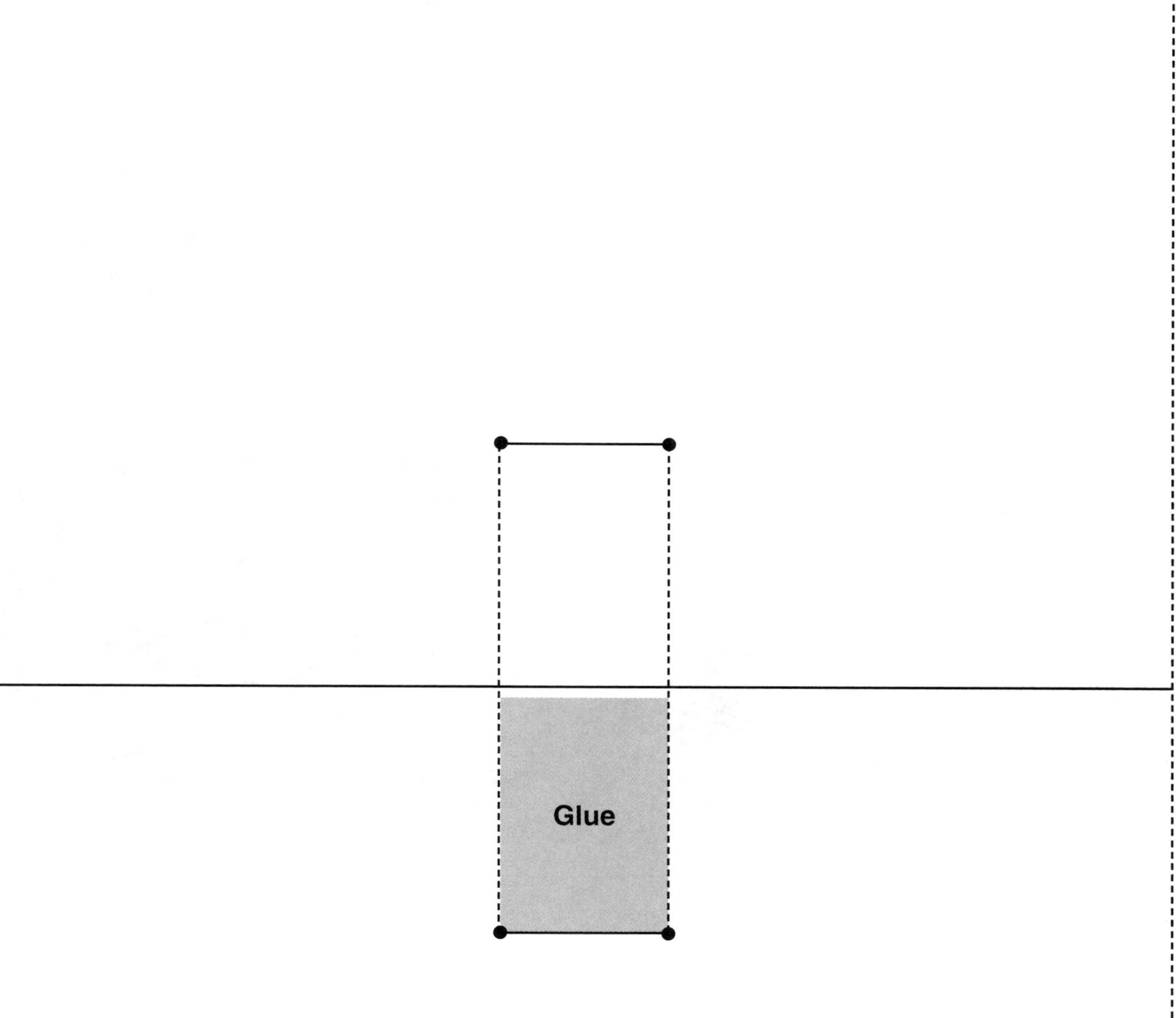

Mr. Washington became a great speaker. He encouraged people to study hard and learn a skill so they would always have a job.

5

Booker T. Washington

Illustrations

page 3 **page 5**

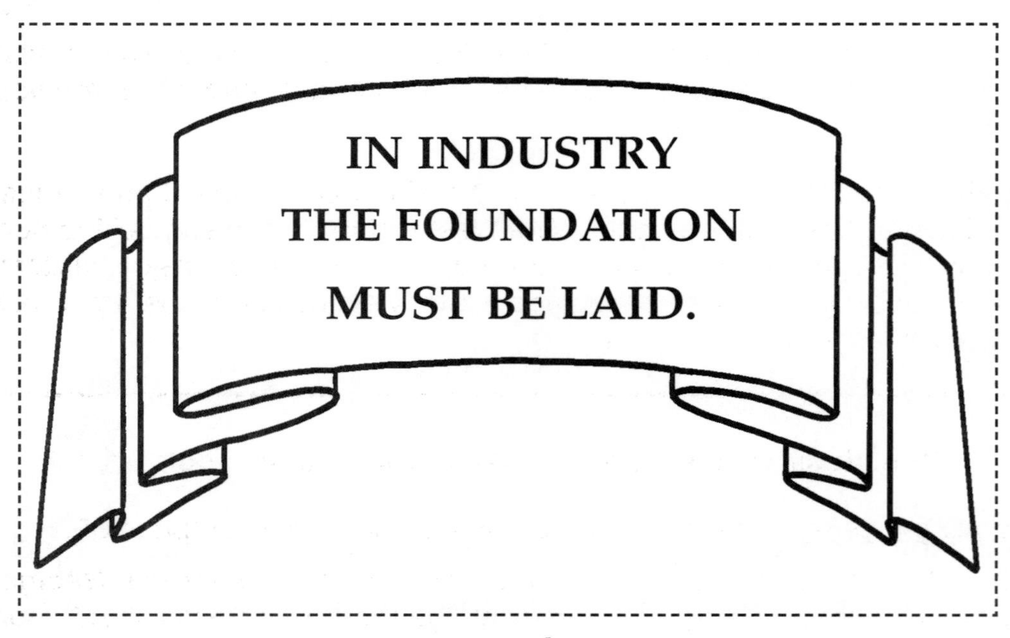

page 4

George Washington

George Washington, known as the "Father of Our Country," was born February 22, 1732, in Virginia. He was interested in history and geography and was particularly good at mathematics. Early in his life, he worked as a surveyor. He saved his money and learned a lot about the land. When he spotted a good tract of land, he purchased it. When George was 21, he joined the army and fought in the French and Indian War. He was a good leader and a brave soldier. In 1759, after the war, he married. He moved his new wife, Martha, and her two children to Mount Vernon to rebuild his half-brother's estate. In 1761, he inherited Mount Vernon in Fairfax County from his half-brother Lawrence's family.

When war broke out between Great Britain and the new American colonies, the Continental Army needed a capable leader. Congress decided that George Washington was the person best suited to lead the troops. He was chosen to be commander-in-chief of the Continental Army in 1775. Washington and his men faced a harsh and bitterly cold winter (1777–1778) at Valley Forge, Pennsylvania. Many battles were lost and many men died before General Washington and his troops were victorious at Yorktown in 1781.

After the war, some people wanted George Washington to be king. But many colonists, including Washington, didn't want their new nation to be ruled by a king. Instead, in 1789, Washington was chosen to be the first president of the United States. He was elected to a second term but refused to run for a third.

According to a legend, a young George Washington chopped down one of his father's cherry trees. When confronted, he said, "I cannot tell a lie. I did cut it with my hatchet." This legend demonstrates Washington's character and the importance he placed on telling the truth. He was respected for his intellect, his sound judgement, and his prudence.

George Washington died on December 14, 1799. He was 76 years old. One of his officers, Henry Lee, said that Washington was "*First in war, first in peace, and first in the hearts of his countrymen*."

The capital of the United States was moved from New York City to the shores of the Potomac and named in George Washington's honor. The Washington monument, built to honor him, was completed in 1884. It is a 555' obelisk covered in white marble. Inside, visitors can view a series of memorial stones set in the walls and travel, via elevator, to the top to take in a breathtaking view of the surrounding area.

Assembly Directions for the *George Washington* Pop-up Book

1. Follow the general directions for pop-up book assembly on page 39.
2. Place the pictures on the pages in the following order: surveyor, George on a horse, Mt. Vernon, George as president, the Washington Monument, money.

George Washington

Map Study

George Washington lived most of his life at Mount Vernon, Virginia. When George was president, the country's capital was in New York. Later, it was moved Washington, D.C., on the shores of the Potomac.

Maryland

Washington D.C.

Kentucky

Mount Vernon

Virginia

Washington, D.C., is the only city of the United States that is not part of a state. Can you find it on the map?

George Washington: Father of Our Country

cover

Page 1

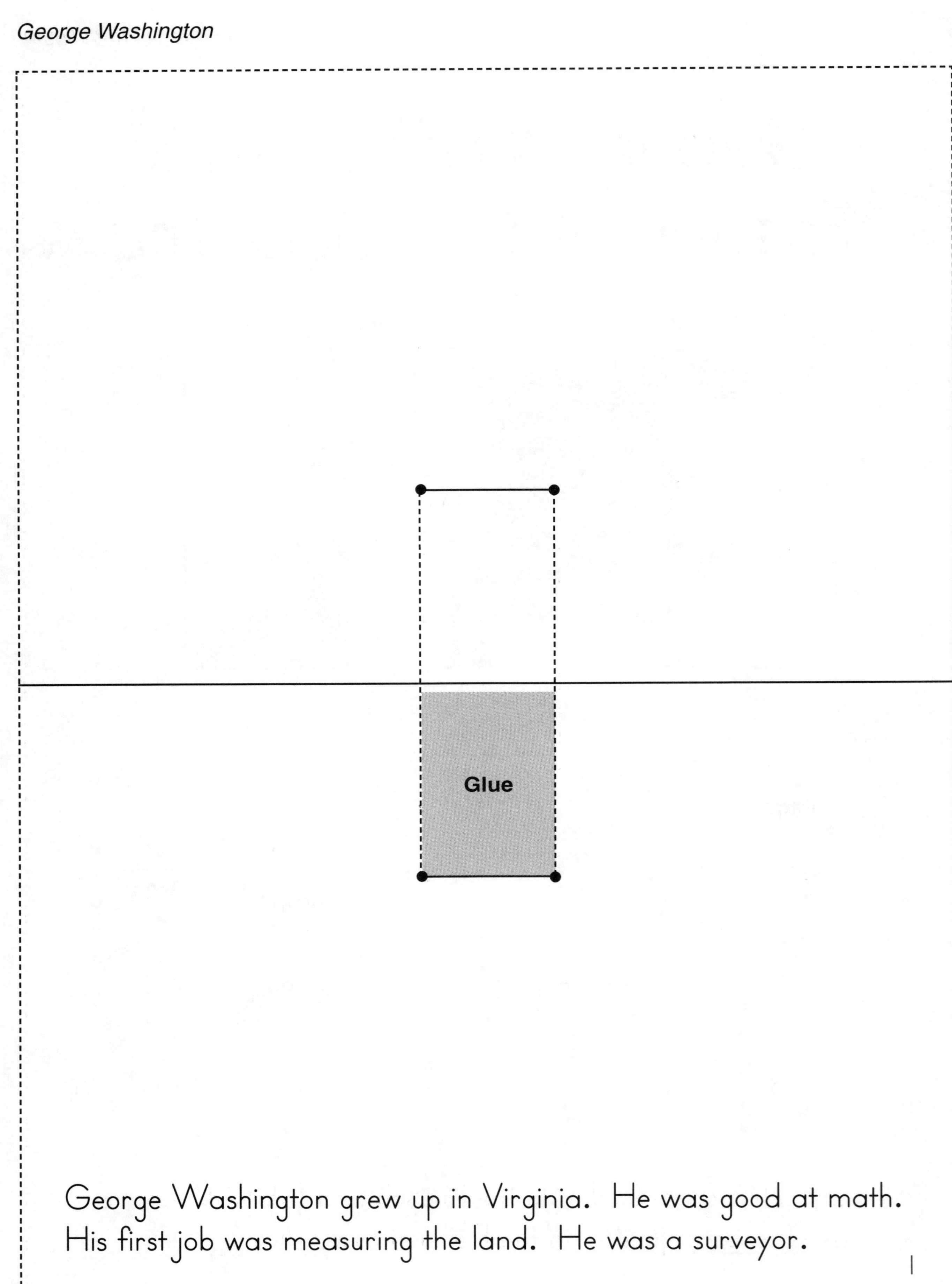

George Washington grew up in Virginia. He was good at math. His first job was measuring the land. He was a surveyor.

1

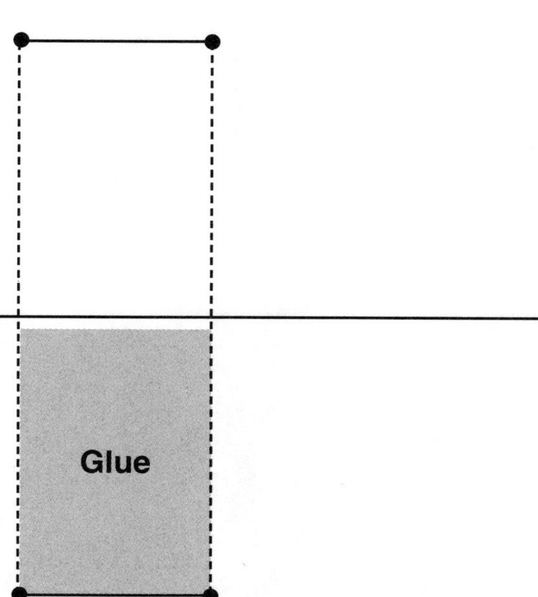

He was such a great soldier in the French and Indian War, he was asked to be a general in the Revolutionary War.

2

Glue

In 1789, George Washington was elected the first president of the United States.

3

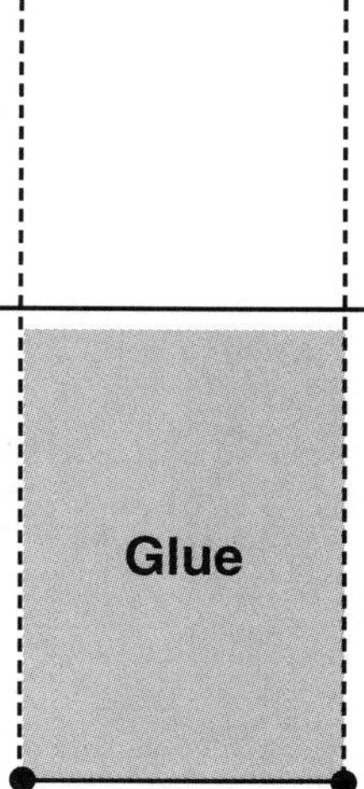

Our nation's capital, Washington, D.C., was named after our first president. In 1884, the Washington Monument was completed in his honor. 4

Glue

George Washington's face is seen on the one-dollar bill and the quarter. He is recognized as the Father of Our Country.

5

Page 2

Page 3

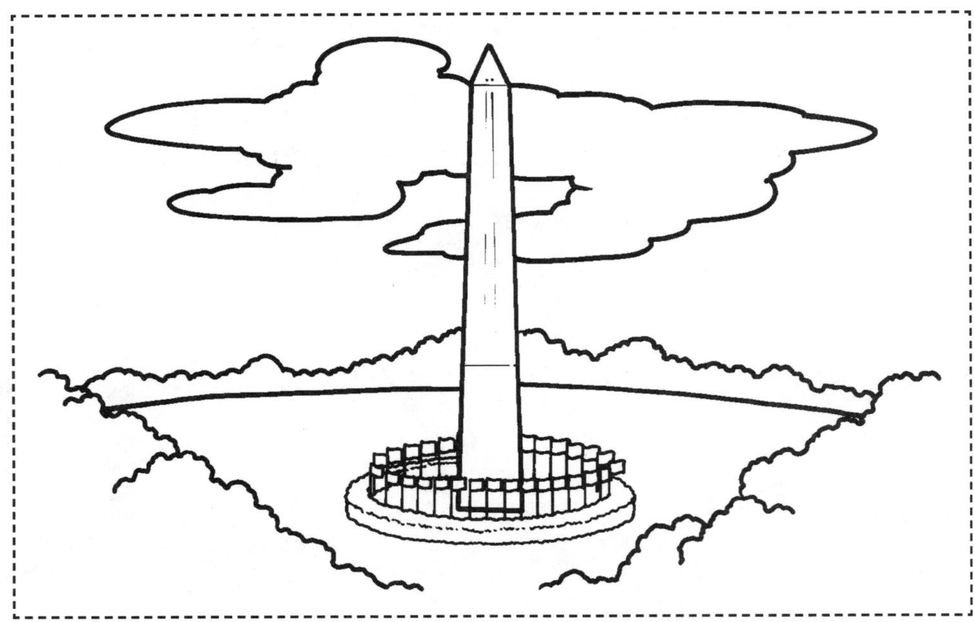

Page 4

THE UNITED STATES
THIS NOTE IS NOT LEGAL TENDER
FOR ANYUSE DEBTS PUBLIC AND PRIVATE
TCM
WASHINGTON, D.C.
ONE
11
11
11
11
Mary Louise Williamson
Treasurer of the United States
Robert W. Smith
Secretary of the Treasury
ONE DOLLAR
LIBERTY
IN GOD WE TRUST
2000

Page 5

Jane Addams

Jane Addams was born in 1860 to a large, wealthy family and lived in Cedarville, Illinois. Her parents were Quakers who supported her desire to get an education, and she was quite ambitious. She was one of the first women of her generation to attend college and was academically, quite successful. After college, she enrolled in medical school, but severe back pain and depression caused her to have to take a leave from her medical studies.

Shortly afterwards, her father died. In 1883, Jane accompanied her stepmother on a visit to Europe where she was able to rest and prepare for a new start. In 1888, she returned to Europe touring with friends. It is on this trip that Jane Addams' eyes were opened to the injustices suffered by the poor, working-class people during the Industrial Revolution.

Jane returned to the United States and observed the same problems in the neighborhoods of Chicago. There, she saw very young children working long hours in factories or playing in garbage piles on the street. She saw women with no childcare working for very low wages. The immigrants residing in Chicago needed assistance, a safe haven, and educational opportunities. Jane resolved to do something about these conditions and create an establishment similar to one she had seen in England called Toynbee Hall.

She and a friend, Ellen Gates Starr, decided to turn a large, old mansion in the community into a safe haven for children and poorer families. The building was called Hull House. It served as a settlement house, in which children could play and learn, and adults could receive education, childcare, and exposure to the arts. Later, social services, legal aid, and medical care were offered there as well.

Jane's leadership skills and her enthusiasm for improving the city rubbed off on churches, colleges, and women's groups. She gained support for her causes and wide recognition. More places like Hull House were created in other cities. She was honored with the Nobel Peace Prize in 1931 for her work as founder of the Settlement House Movement.

Jane Addams enjoyed the chance to be and do something more. Her work at Hull House was only one facet of her career. She was a published author, a founding member of the NAACP and the ACLU, and a suffragette. She remains highly respected and serves as an inspiration to people to this day.

Assembly Directions for the *Jane Addams* Pop-up Book

1. Follow the general directions for pop-up book assembly on page 39.
2. Place the pictures on the pages in the following order: Jane Addams; poor, unhappy children; Hull House; clean, happy children playing inside; Nobel Peace Prize.

Jane Addams

Map Study

Jane Addams' established Hull House in Chicago, Illinois.

Jane Addams: Protector of the Poor

Cover

Page 1

Page 3

Glue

During the late 1800s, most women were wives and mothers and did not work outside the home. Jane Addams wanted a different life. She was an educated woman who wanted to make a difference in her world.

1

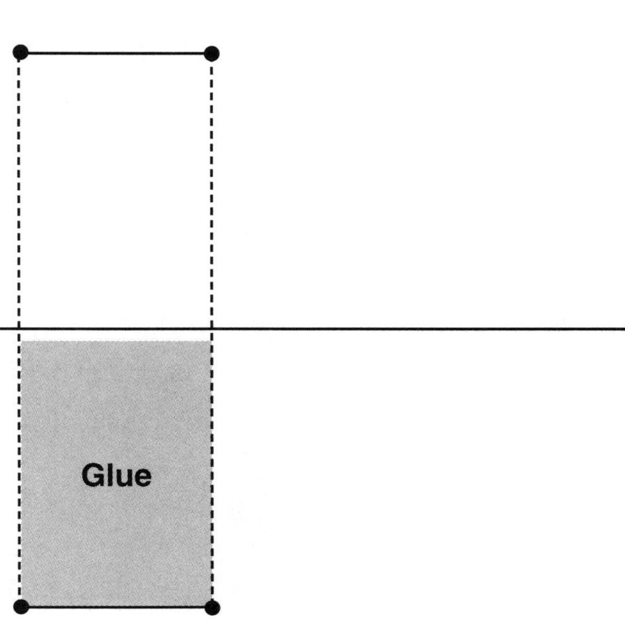

Jane Addams saw poor, dirty children playing in garbage in the streets of Chicago. She knew they needed help and a nice place to play.

2

Glue

She found a mansion and fixed it up. It was called Hull House.

3

Children played there instead of in the streets. Poor people came there when they had no place else to go.

4

Glue

In 1931, Jane Addams won the Nobel Peace Prize for all her hard work on behalf of women, children, and the poor.

5

Page 2

Page 5

Page 4

Betsy Ross

Betsy Ross was born in Philadelphia in 1752. She was a seamstress who shared an upholstery business in Philadelphia with her husband, John. When John was killed in an explosion in 1776, Betsy continued to run the business at the upholstery shop against the advice of her father.

Nearly 100 years later at a historical society meeting, Mrs. Ross's grandson, William J. Canby, first told what has become a famous story about his grandmother. He first remembered hearing the story when he was 11 and his grandmother was about 84 years old. He recollected that his grandmother told him that General George Washington asked her to make a flag for the country. General Washington suggested a design of 13 stars and 13 stripes. His stars had six points. Betsy made a beautiful five-pointed star by folding a piece of paper and making one snip. George was impressed. Five-pointed stars it would be! Betsy placed all 13 stars in a circle. The 13 stars and 13 stripes represented the 13 colonies existing at the time. The stars-and-stripes design was adopted by Congress on June 14, 1777.

For years and years, historians have searched government records and George Washington's writings in order to substantiate the information handed down within the Ross family. They have been unable to prove the legend. They have found, however, evidence to indicate that Betsy Ross did make flags for the Pennsylvania state ships.

Other descendants of Betsy Ross wrote the 1909 book, *The Evolution of the American Flag*. In the book, there is a picture of a painting showing Betsy Ross at a meeting of the committee of Congress. There are no records of this meeting. The artist, Charles H. Weisgerber, may have been speculating about what actually happened. The models he used were descendants of Betsy Ross. A flag with a circle of stars is shown in the painting. Photographs of that painting were later used in school textbooks, making any untruths difficult to dispel.

Many believe that there is no reason that Betsy, a Quaker, would have been making up stories about her life to tell her grandchildren. Quakers value modesty and truthfulness. More than one descendant remembers Betsy's stories, and the retellings are very consistent with each other.

During the war, there may not have been time to make clear records of every meeting that took place. However, one story tells of a fellow church member's visit to Betsy Ross's shop after her meeting with the Congressional committee. The visitor saw the star that Betsy had cut for them, and he asked to keep it. In 1925, his family safe was opened to reveal that same star. It is now on exhibit at the Free Quaker Meeting House in Philadelphia.

Whatever the truth may be, most people enjoy the story of Betsy Ross and the making of the flag. As a result, it has become part of our history.

Betsy Ross

Map Study

Betsy Ross lived and worked in Philadelphia, Pennsylvania.

Putting Together *Betsy Ross*

Materials

For each student you will need:

- four sheets of white paper
- one 9" x 12" sheet of red construction paper
- one template for stars
- text strips
- dark blue crayon or marker
- 13 stars (Use star stickers or cuts from a star hole punch.)
- scissors and glue

Preparation for the *Betsy Ross* Layered Book

1. Three of the four white pages used in this book may need to be precut for students. The pages should measure as follows: 4 1/2" x 11", 5 3/4" x 11", and 7" x 11". The last page should be trimmed 1/4" from the top to measure 8 1/4" x 11".

   Options: Give students four 8 1/2" x 11" pieces of copy paper and have them measure and cut the pieces of paper themselves. Or create templates by marking a dashed line on each piece of white paper for each of the four measurements. Make copies of these sheets and have children cut each sheet on the dashed line. A third option would be to precut the sheets of paper and hand them out, ready-to-use.
2. Trim the red paper to 9" x 11". To create the red stripes for the flag, cut the trimmed sheet into seven equal strips, each measuring 5/8" x 11".

Assembly Directions for the *Betsy Ross* Layered Book

Top Page

1. Glue a red stripe to the top of the 4 ½" x 11" sheet; glue a second stripe at the bottom of the sheet. Evenly space two more stripes in between them.
2. Color the template blue or use a 4 ½" x 5" piece of blue construction paper.
3. Place the stars on the template as shown.

Pages 2–4

1. Glue one red stripe to the bottom of each page.
2. Layer the book with the largest page on the bottom and the smallest page on top.
3. Make sure that the tops and left sides of the pages are lined up evenly. Red and white stripes should be visible all the way down the flag. Double-check for 13 stripes.
4. Staple down the left side of the flag.
5. Place the text strips on the pages so they do not show when the book is closed. Add the picture of Betsy Ross to page 4.

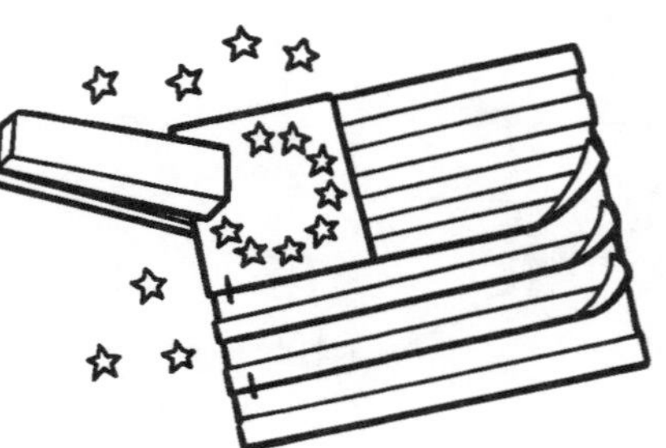

Betsy Ross

Text for the *Betsy Ross* Layered Book

Betsy Ross was a seamstress.

2

General George Washington asked her to make a flag for our new country.

3

She made a red, white, and blue flag. It had 13 stars and 13 stripes which stood for the 13 colonies.

4

Template for Flag Stars

Page 4

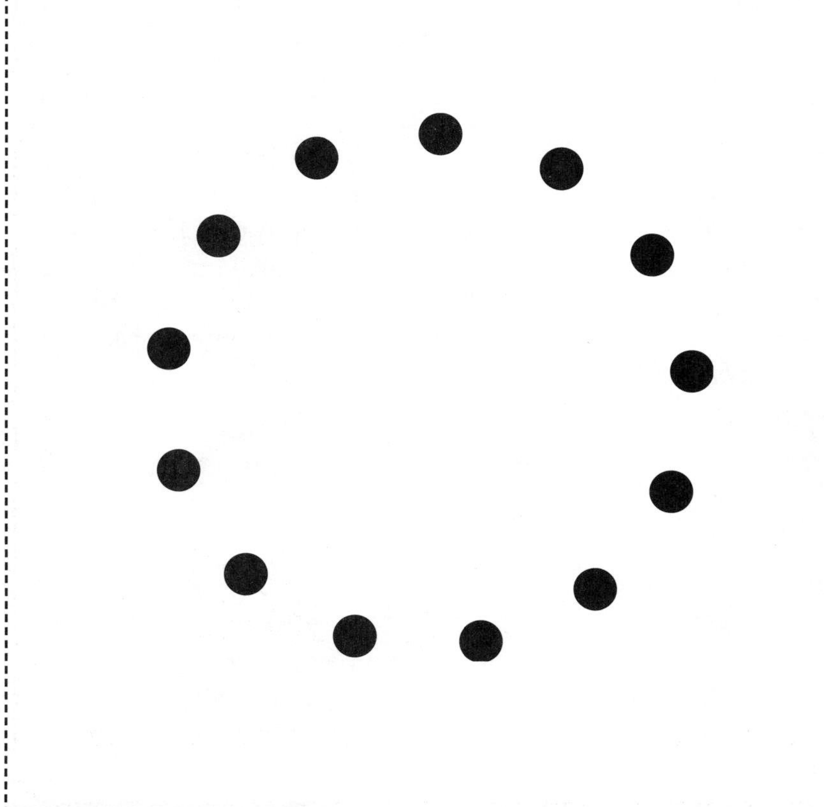

Davy Crockett

Davy Crockett is a legendary figure in the history of the United States. He is known for his frontier experiences and for his oratory skills. Davy Crockett was born in east Tennessee on August 17, 1786. His family was poor, and life on the frontier was not easy. Creek and Cherokee Native Americans killed his grandparents before he was born. Because Davy was from a poor pioneer family, he did not have the opportunity for a formal education. It is said that he began his formal education at age 13 but that it did not last long. He needed to work and preferred being out of doors.

When Davy was 12, his father, a tavern owner, made a plan with another man for Davy to help drive the man's cattle to Virginia. The man kept Davy and forced him to work longer than the time agreed upon by his father. Davy escaped during a snowstorm and returned home to his family. He helped work off the family debt by working for men to whom his father owed money. It was during this time that he became an excellent marksman. He borrowed his employers' rifles and practiced shooting whenever he could.

Davy married twice. He and his first wife, Polly Finley, had three children. Crockett was an army scout at the time. He served with bravery under Andrew Jackson in the Creek Indian War. Sadly, Polly died in 1815. In 1816, Davy married Elizabeth Patton, a widow with two children. During this period of his life, he became known for his storytelling. He told many tall tales involving bears and Native Americans. Townspeople loved to listen to him retell and embellish his hunting exploits. He also became interested in politics at this time.

Crockett was a charismatic speaker known for his sense of humor. These traits served him well in the political arena. He was first elected colonel of the state militia and later served two terms in the Tennessee legislature. It was said that he killed 105 bears between the two legislative sessions from 1822–1823. Davy Crockett was elected in 1827 to the United States Congress. He served three terms in Congress where he was easily recognized by his coonskin cap. Disagreements on policy led Davy out of politics. David Crockett wrote his autobiography in 1834, called *A Narrative of the Life of David Crockett of the State of Tennessee.*

Davy Crockett left politics and traveled to Texas where he hoped to become a land owner. In 1835, he fought for Texas' independence from Mexico. Crockett and his men defended the Alamo for several days until their ammunition ran out. He was killed there on March 6, 1836. His efforts were noble and Texas was able to win freedom soon after the battle at the Alamo.

Assembly Directions for the *Davy Crockett* Layered Book

Materials: Copy of the cover, one half sheet (6½" x 9") each of green, dark brown, tan, and light blue paper, text strips, template pages, and a 2" x 6½" piece of faux fur (optional)

1. Cut out the cover and each template.
2. Trace the Alamo onto the tan paper, the bear onto the dark brown paper, and the forest onto the green paper. Use the light blue paper for the sky (back cover).
3. Cut out each piece of construction paper. Layer from back to front as follows: blue, tan, brown, and green, cover. Make sure left and bottom edges are together. Staple down the side of the booklet. *Optional:* Attach the fur strip to the left side, over the staples.
4. Cut out each line of text and glue it to the corresponding page.

Davy Crockett

Map Study

Davy Crockett was born in Tennessee and died at the Alamo in San Antonio, Texas.

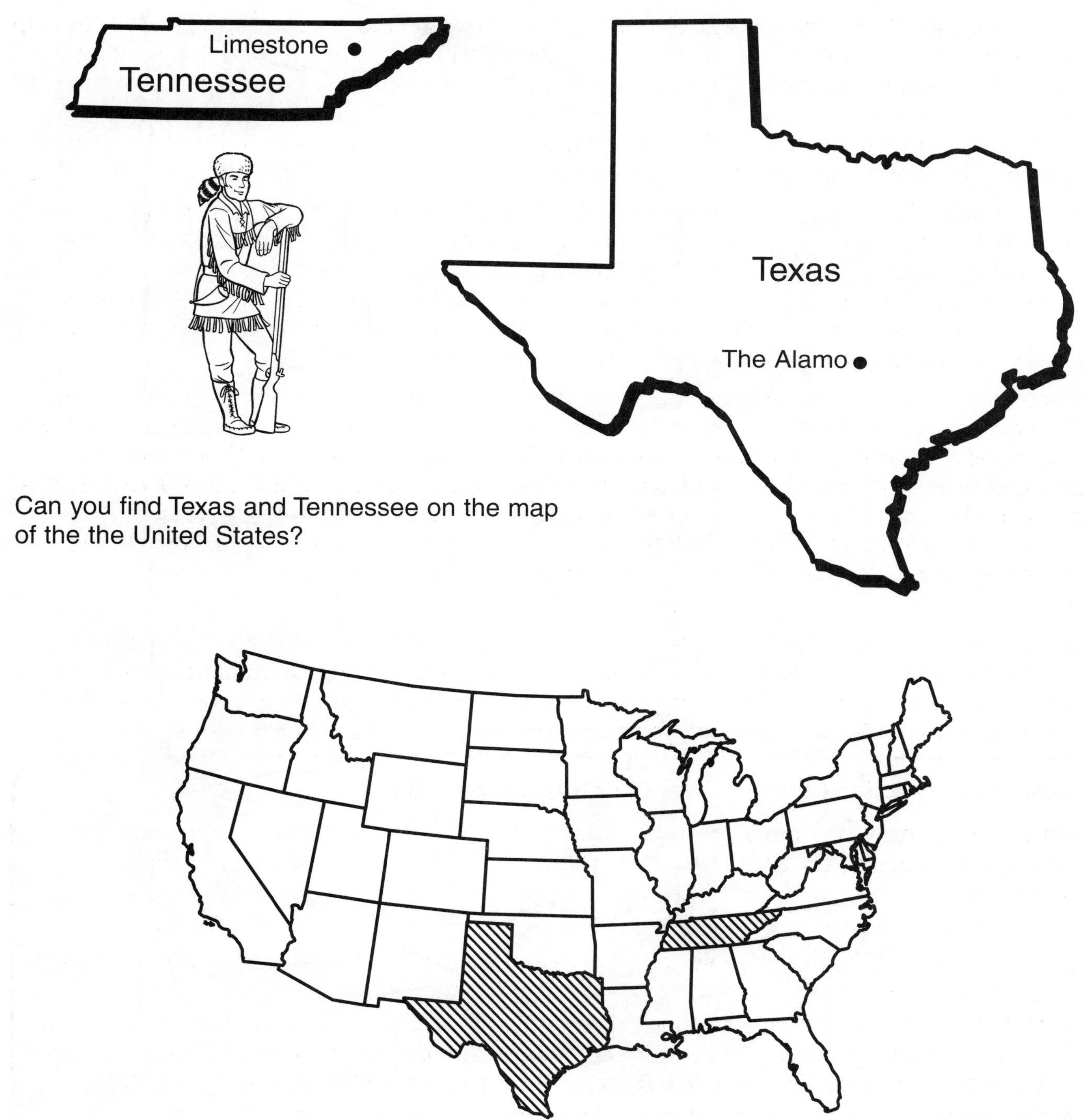

Can you find Texas and Tennessee on the map of the the United States?

Davy Crockett
Frontiersman
1786–1836

Template for the Alamo

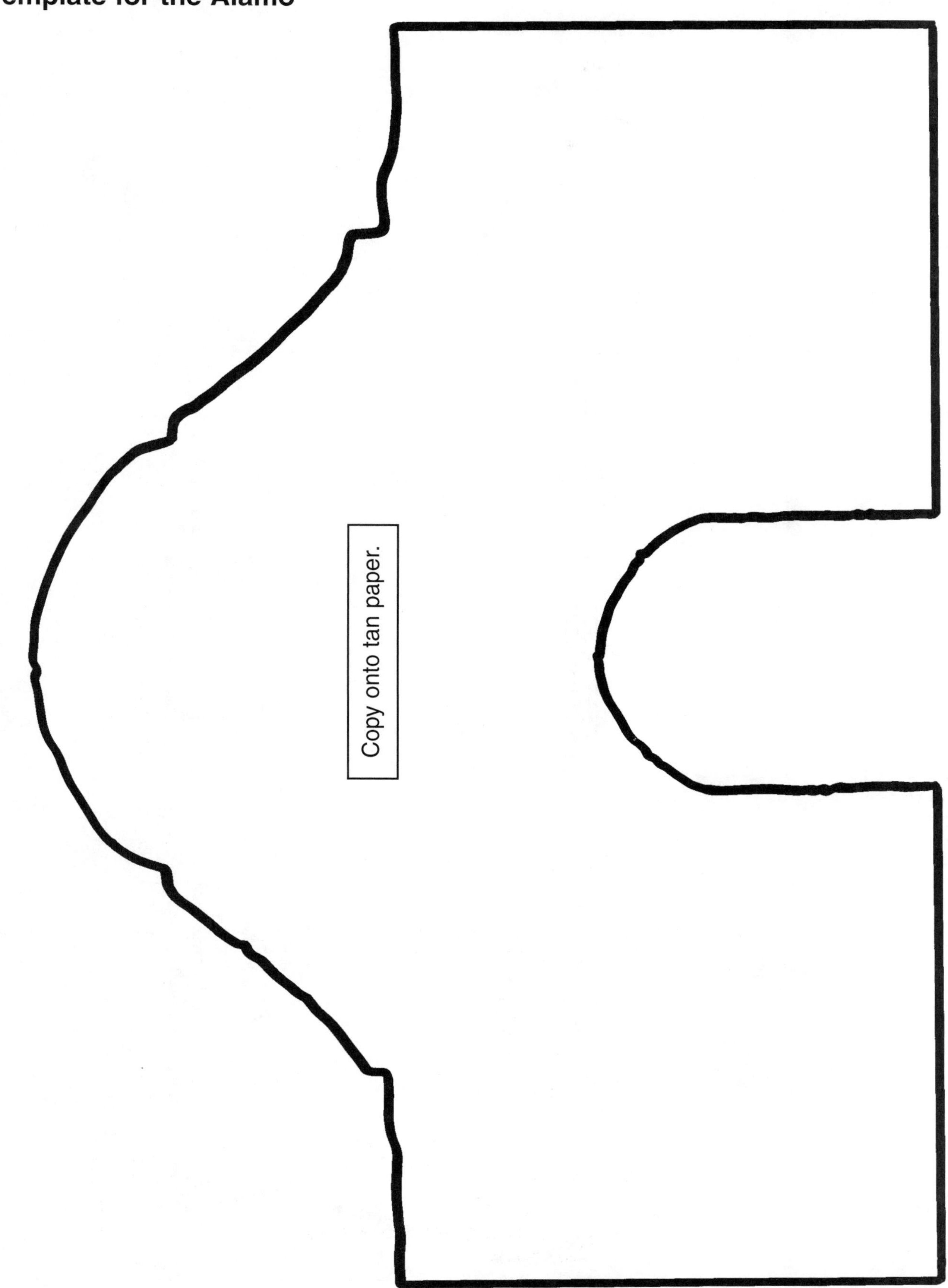

Template for the bear

Template for the forest

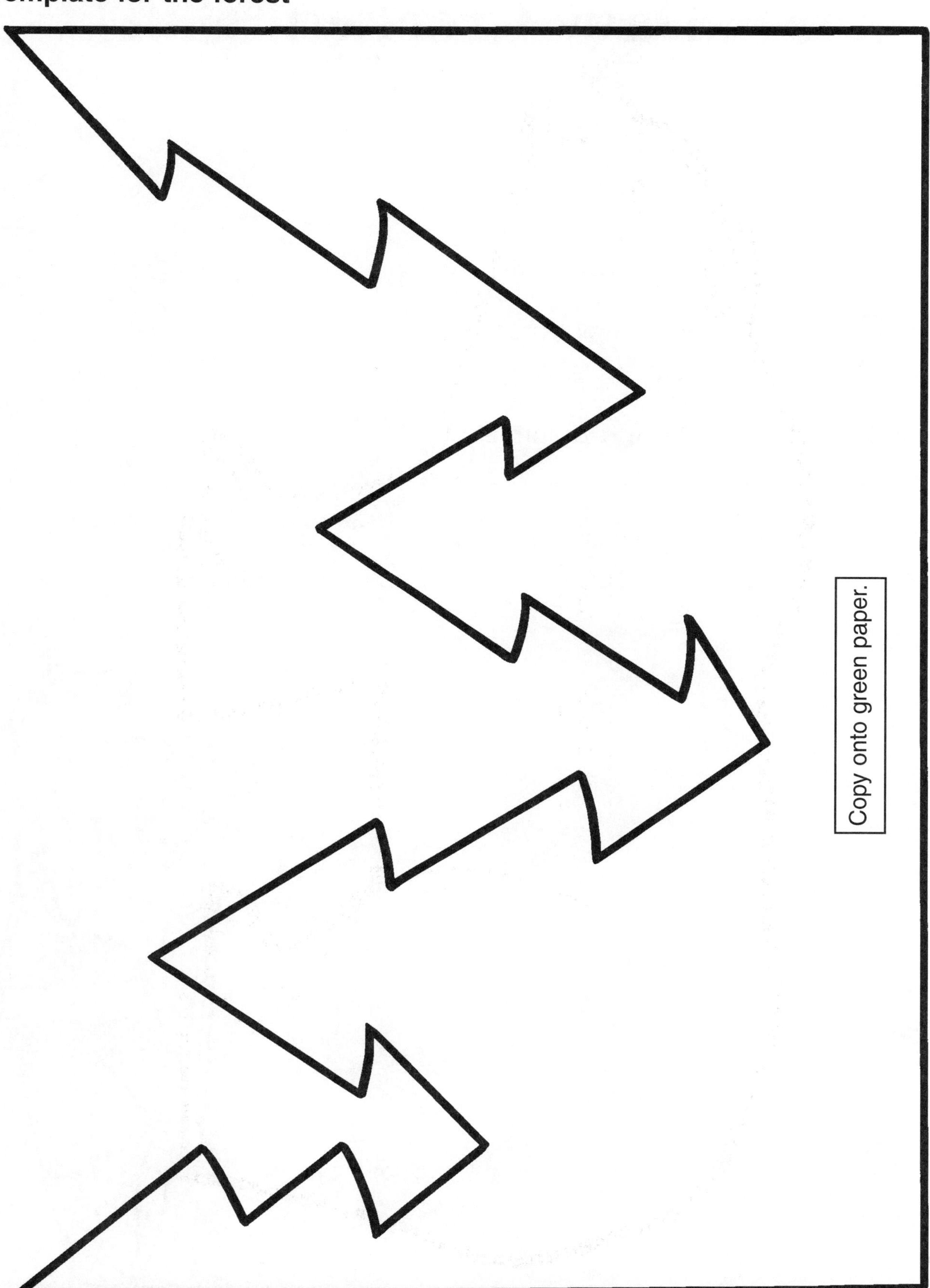

Davy Crockett

Davy Crockett explored new lands. 1

He was a bear hunter and a soldier. 2

He died fighting in a war at The Alamo in Texas. 3

Christopher Columbus

Christopher Columbus was born in Genoa, Italy, in 1451. Genoa was an important seaport at the time and Columbus' father encouraged him to enter the trading business. Columbus sailed on trading ships and later drew and sold maps with his brother. Europeans of the time sought gold, gems, silk, and spices, including nutmeg, cloves, and mace that came from the East. These riches had previously been brought to Europe by costly overland caravans. Many adventurers sought newer, faster routes to the East. Columbus reasoned that if he kept sailing west from Spain or Portugal, he would eventually reach Asia by boat.

Late in the fifteenth century, Christopher Columbus approached King Ferdinand and Queen Isabella of Spain with his plan to reach India without having to sail around Africa. He was determined to find a new trade route. It took Ferdinand and Isabella five years to agree to finance the search for a new sea route to Asia. They promised Columbus honors and a percentage of the trade resulting from this route.

Columbus set sail in 1492 with three ships, 90 crewmembers, and a bold plan. Columbus used the North Star as his guide and a compass to plot his course. After a little over two months at sea, Columbus landed in North America. Thinking it was India, he named the native people Indians. He and his crews explored many harbors in the Caribbean Sea but did not find the riches they had sought. The *Niña* and the *Pinta* returned to Spain in 1493. The *Santa Maria* had crashed into a rock in the Caribbean and some of its crew remained on the island at the fort they had constructed. Columbus was financed for more voyages despite the lack of trade items he returned with after the first journey.

Columbus was credited with discovering America for hundreds of years. We now know that other Europeans such as Leif Ericson arrived in 1000 A.D., well before Columbus. Although he never found the route he was looking for, Columbus' persistence did open the New World to further European exploration and eventual settlement.

The second Monday of October is recognized as Columbus Day. Citizens of the United States acknowledge Christopher Columbus's incredible voyage on three small ships named the *Niña*, the *Pinta*, and the *Santa Maria*.

Christopher Columbus

Map Study

Columbus's first journey to America.

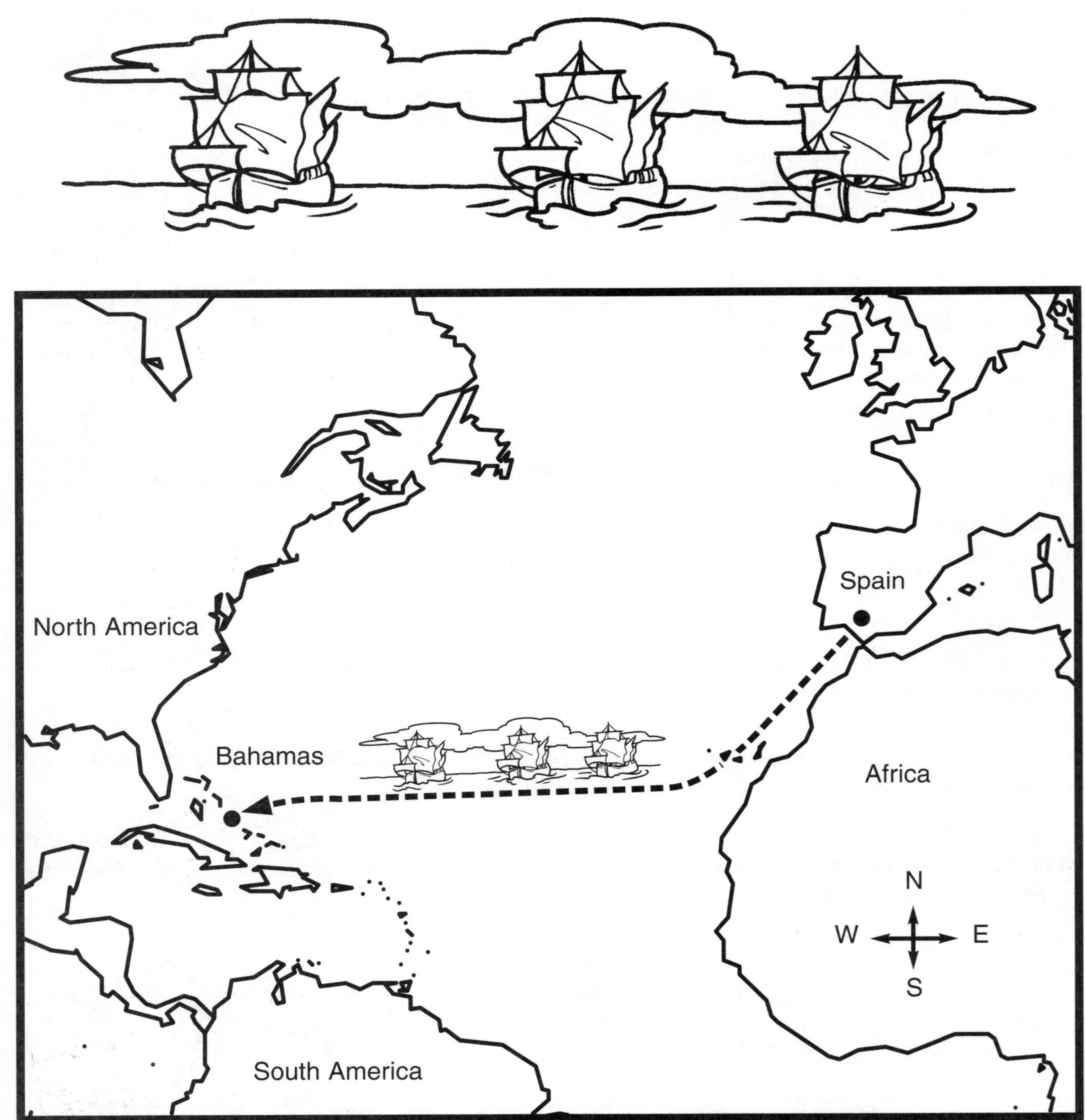

Putting Together *Christopher Columbus*

Materials

- One sheet, 6½" x 9", each of light blue, dark blue, green, white, and brown construction paper
- copy of each template (pages 96, 97, 98)
- copy of the text page (page 98)
- stapler
- red felt pen or crayon

Pre-assembly Preparation

Choose one option.

- Run copies of each page on white paper for the students and have them color each part with the colors suggested below.
- Create templates on cardboard or tagboard for students to use to trace the shapes on colored paper. Make the small rectangle and the waves on dark blue, the boat on brown, and the island on green.
- Copy the templates onto the correct color construction paper.

Assembly Directions for the *Christopher Columbus* Layered Book

1. Cut out the templates, sails, and text stripes.
2. Glue the dark blue rectangle to the bottom end of the light blue rectangle, matching the bottom corners.
3. Glue the green island to the center of the dark blue rectangle.
4. Center and staple the sail to the light blue sky, making the edges even. Staple the dark blue waves across the bottom of the dark blue part of the rectangle.
5. Fold the waves down. Position the boat so that it can be stapled at the left side of the rectangle and will not be inhibited by the waves.
6. Attach the text as follows: Fold the waves down and glue page 1 to the back of them. Fold back the boat and glue page 2 to the back of it. Lift the sails and glue page 3 to the back of the sails.
7. Color the cross on the sail red.

Templates for the ocean

Templates for the island and the ship

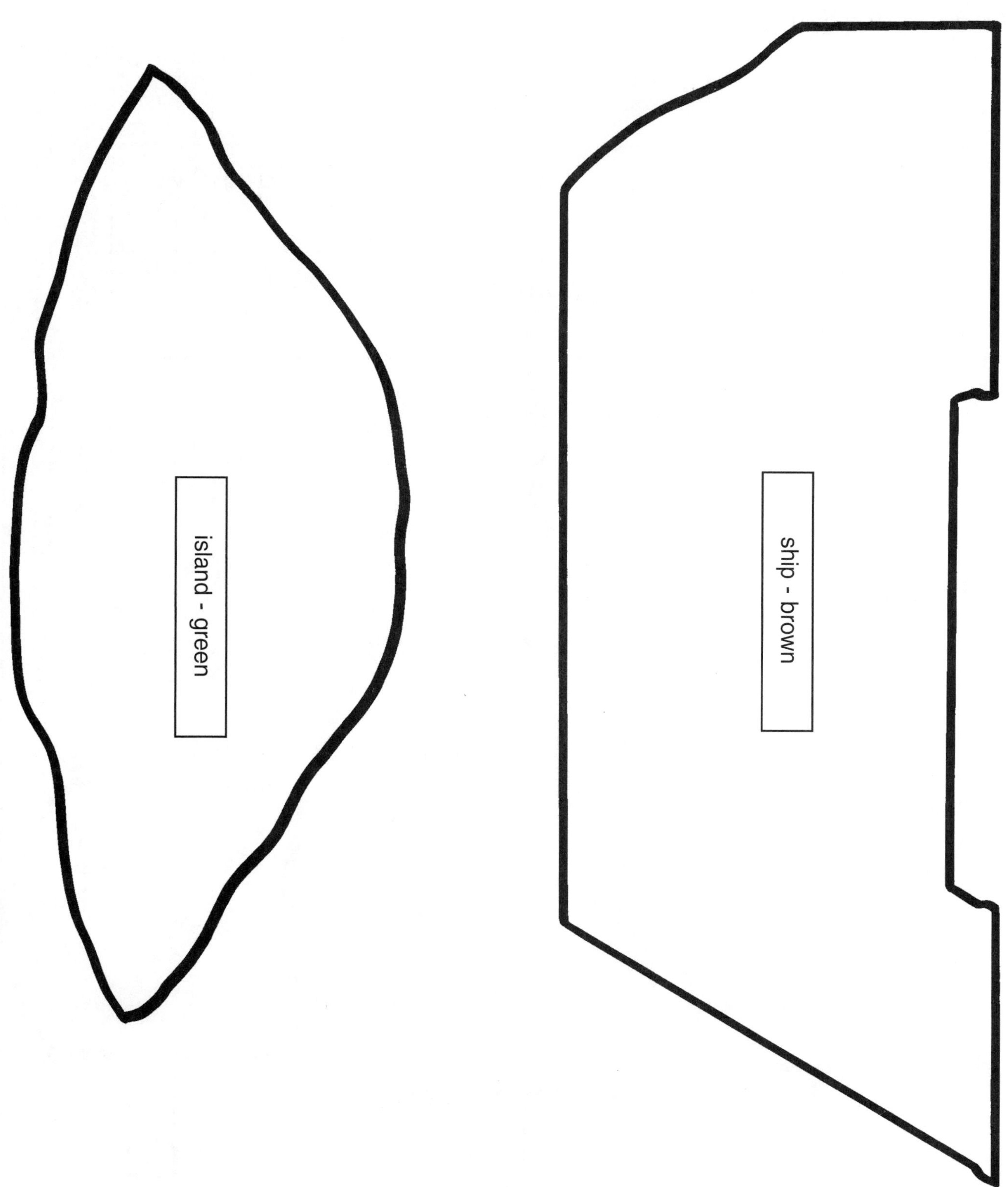

Christopher Columbus

Text

Columbus sailed west in August 1492 to find gold and spices in the Indies. 1

He took three Spanish ships named the *Niña*, the *Pinta*, and the *Santa Maria*. 2

He discovered America on October 12, 1492. 3

Sails

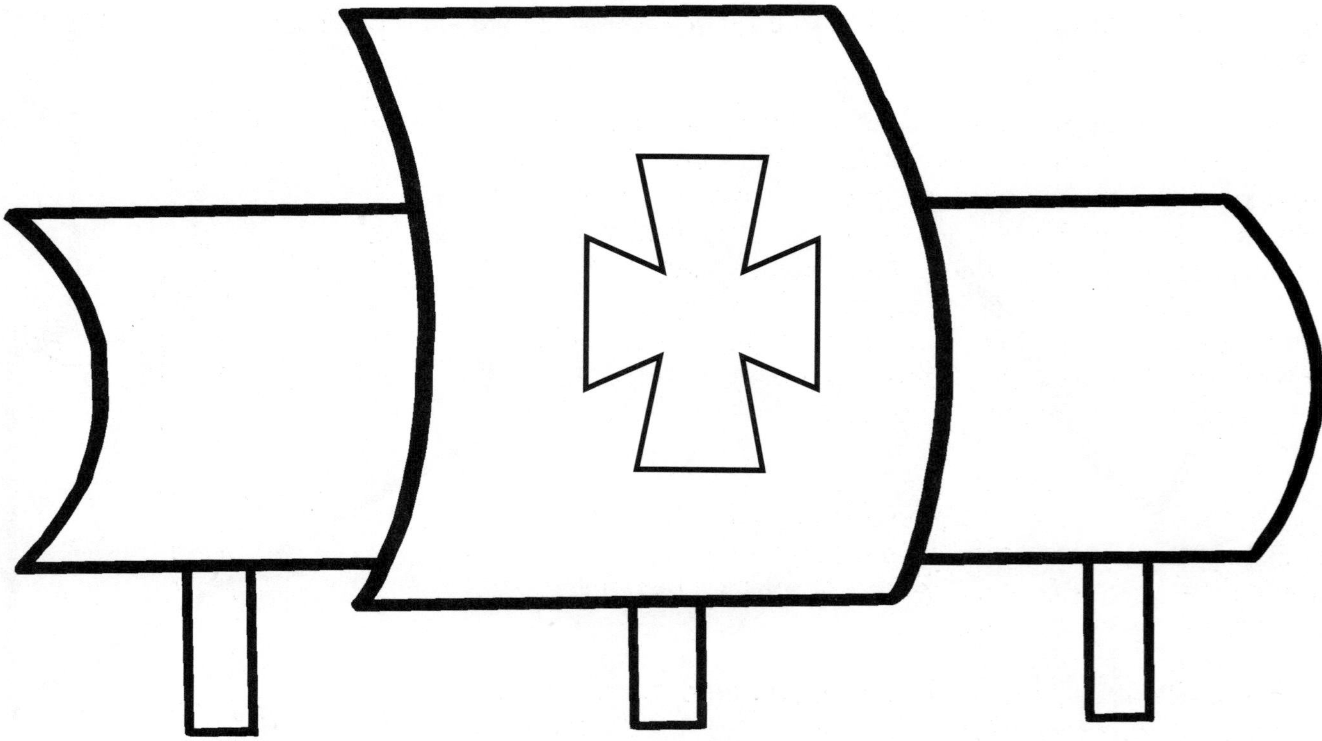

Abraham Lincoln

Abraham Lincoln was born on February 12, 1809, in a little log cabin in the backwoods of Kentucky. Lincoln once said that he went to school by "the littles"—a little now and a little then. He loved to read and eagerly read everything he could get his hands on.

When Abraham Lincoln was 21, his family moved to Illinois. He helped his parents build their new house, plow and plant their fields, and build more rail fences. When he was 22, he left his family to be on his own. In 1836 Lincoln took a test to become a lawyer. He moved to Springfield, the new capital of Illinois, and practiced law. In 1842 he married Mary Todd, and four years later he was elected to Congress.

In 1858 Abraham Lincoln was the Republican candidate for the Senate. Though not an abolitionist, he was against slavery, a practice he had seen years before while visiting New Orleans. Lincoln ran against Stephen Douglas, and though he did not win, their debates made him famous. He was devoted to the cause of personal freedom for all people. Abraham Lincoln was elected the sixteenth president of the United States in 1860. He was the first Republican to become president.

In 1861, the southern states withdrew from the United States and formed the Confederate States of America. The South depended on slaves for their economy, and the North did not believe in slavery. The Civil War broke out, and Lincoln supported keeping the Union intact. On January 1, 1863, he signed the Emancipation Proclamation, freeing all the slaves. Later that year, he gave one of his most famous speeches at Gettysburg, Pennsylvania, declaring that "government of the people, by the people, for the people, shall not perish from the earth."

The war ended just as Lincoln was beginning his second term as President. Within days of his inauguration, while he was attending a play at Ford's Theater, Abraham Lincoln was shot and killed.

He is considered by many to have been one of our greatest presidents. He served during a particularly difficult time in our country and fought for the equality of all men.

Abraham Lincoln

Map Study

Abraham Lincoln was born in Kentucky and lived most of his life in Illinois.

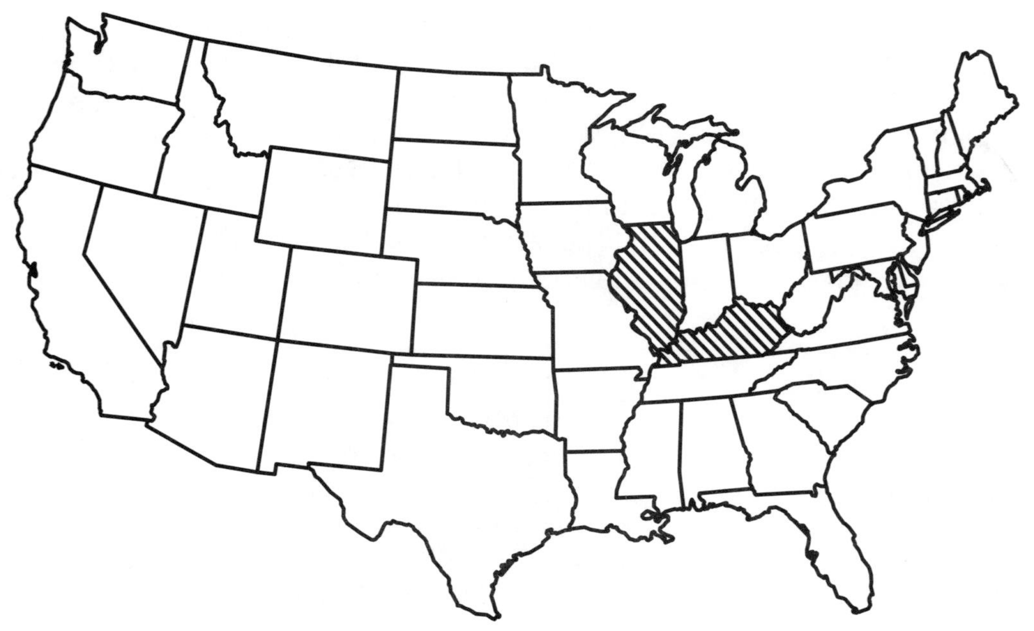

Putting Together *Abraham Lincoln*

Materials

- two black sheets of construction paper (9" x12")
- one tan (manila) sheet (9" x12")
- copy of the text strips
- scissors

Directions for the *Abraham Lincoln* Layered Book

1. Make the copies of the templates on card stock.
2. Cut out the templates, then trace them on construction paper as follows: beard, hair, and hat on black paper, and face on manila paper.
3. Cut out each piece for the book, then layer as follows: face, beard, hair, and hat.
4. Place one staple on the left side of the face where the face, beard, hair, and hat intersect.
5. Attach page 1 to back of hat, page 2 under the hair, and page 3 under beard.

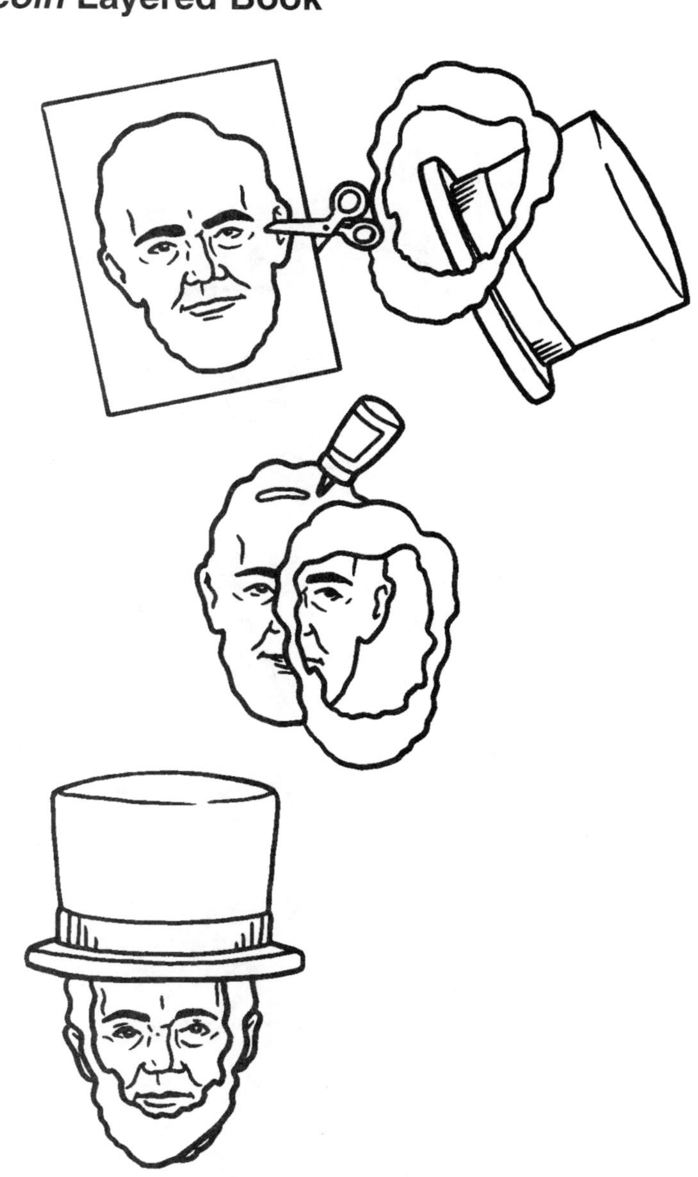

Abraham Lincoln

Face Template

Copy onto manila paper

Abraham Lincoln

Copy onto black or brown paper.

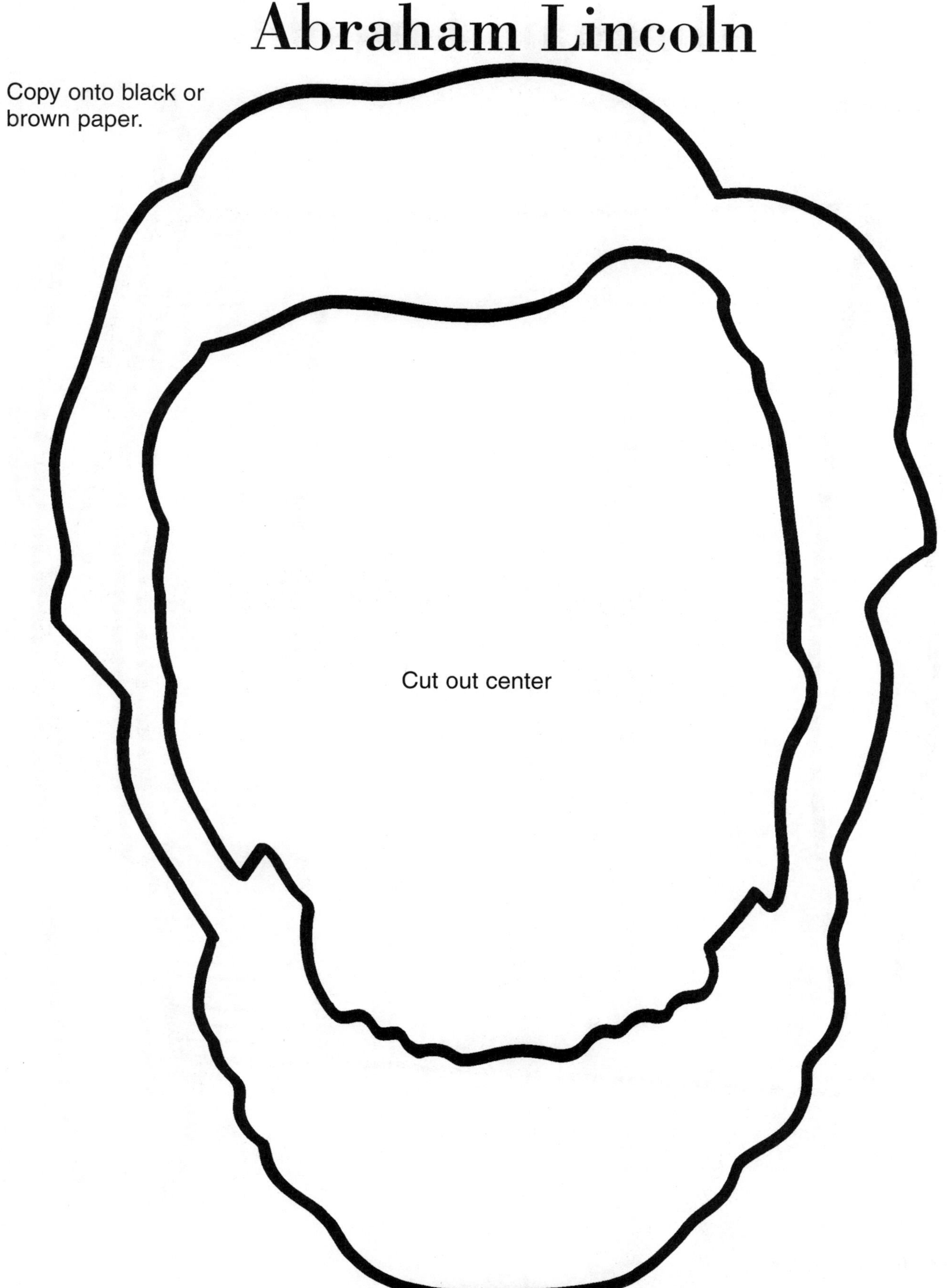

Abraham Lincoln

Template for hat

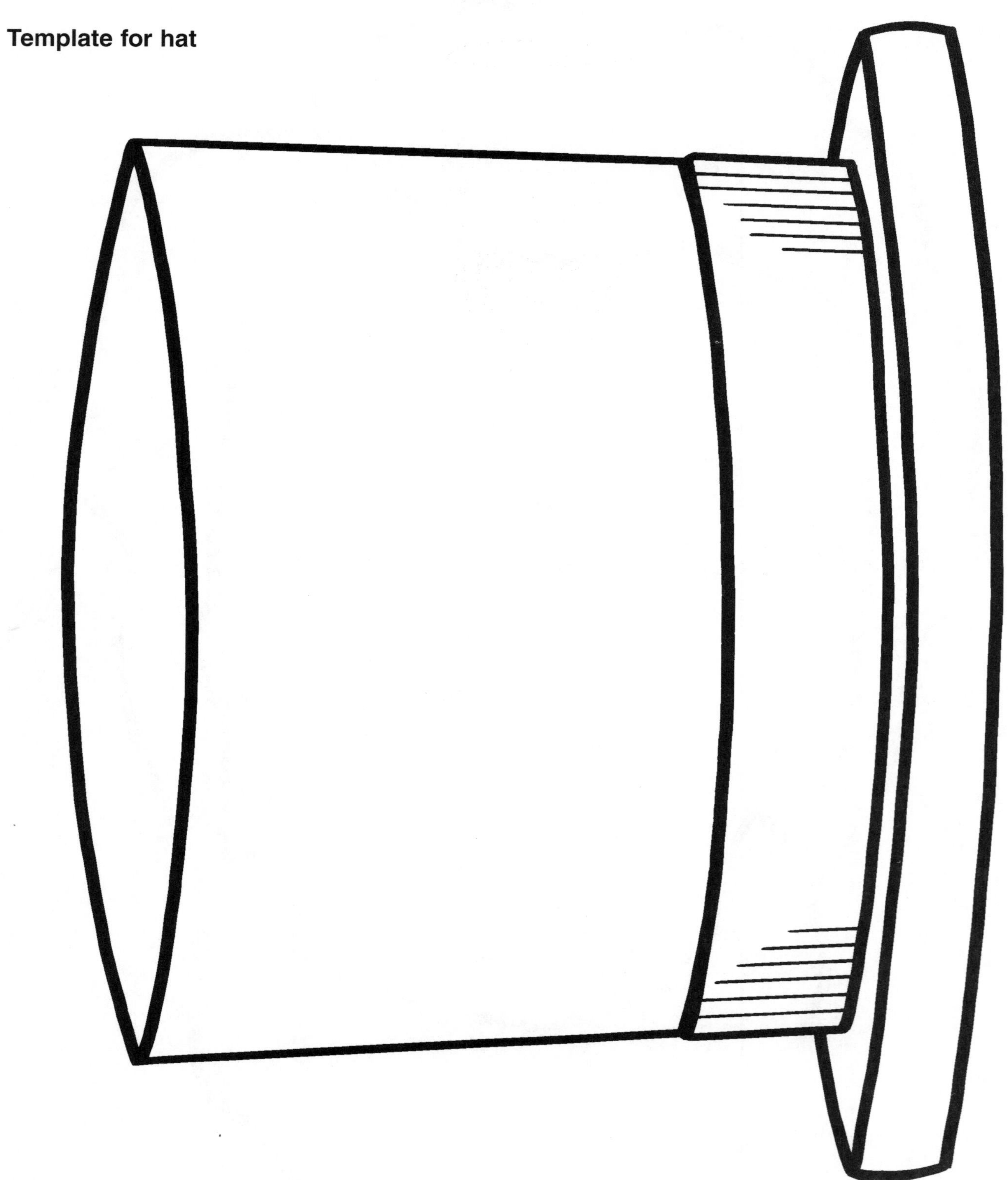

Copy onto black paper.

Abraham Lincoln

Text for Abraham Lincoln

Abraham Lincoln wore a stovepipe hat in which he kept important papers. 1

He was raised as a poor farmer but was smart enough to become a lawyer when he grew up. 2

Abraham Lincoln was the 16th president in 1860. He freed the slaves. 3

George Washington Carver

George Washington Carver was the son of slave parents. When he was very young, they were kidnapped and he never saw them again. He was raised by his plantation owners on a farm in Diamond Grove, Missouri. Early on, George was interested in all kinds of plants. He worked hard to make a place for himself in school. He was accepted at Simpson College. There he continued to focus on the study and drawing of plants. He went on to Iowa Agricultural College, which is now Iowa State University, to get his degree. After graduation, he stayed on to attain his M.S. in agriculture.

Booker T. Washington invited him to teach at the Tuskegee Institute in Alabama. There, George created an agricultural science laboratory where he and the students conducted experiments on various crops and soil nutrients. He wanted to create high crop yield. He figured out that crop rotation would make soil last much longer, so he planted peas and peanuts in a field one year, then put cotton in that field the next. This way, the soil in the cotton field could be replenished every other year with nutrients that the peanuts and peas had put back into the soil.

George spent a lot of time developing uses for the peanut, the sweet potato, and the pecan. For example, he used peanuts to make chocolate-coated peanuts, peanut brittle, and salad oil. He made unusual things, too, like paint, peanut sausage, peanut punch, tan remover, peanut tofu sauce, soap, sizing for walls, axle grease, shaving cream, and wood filler. There seemed to be no end to what Carver could do with a peanut. He brought new respect to the field of agriculture. He is honored at the Carver Memorial Museum at Tuskegee University and at his birthplace in Diamond Grove.

Putting Together the *George Washington Carver* Lift-tab Book

Materials

- copies of the text pages (pages 108–110)
- copies of lift tab pages (pages 111–112)
- scissors
- glue
- stapler
- markers or crayons

Assembly Directions

1. Color the book pages and the matching flaps.
2. Fold each page on the dotted line.
3. Put the pages in numerical order and staple them on the left side.
4. Cut out the flaps and glue each to the page at the star(s).
5. Color the flaps to match the rest of the picture.

George Washington Carver

Map Study

George Washington Carver was born in Diamond Grove, Missouri. He did important work at the Tuskegee Institute in Alabama.

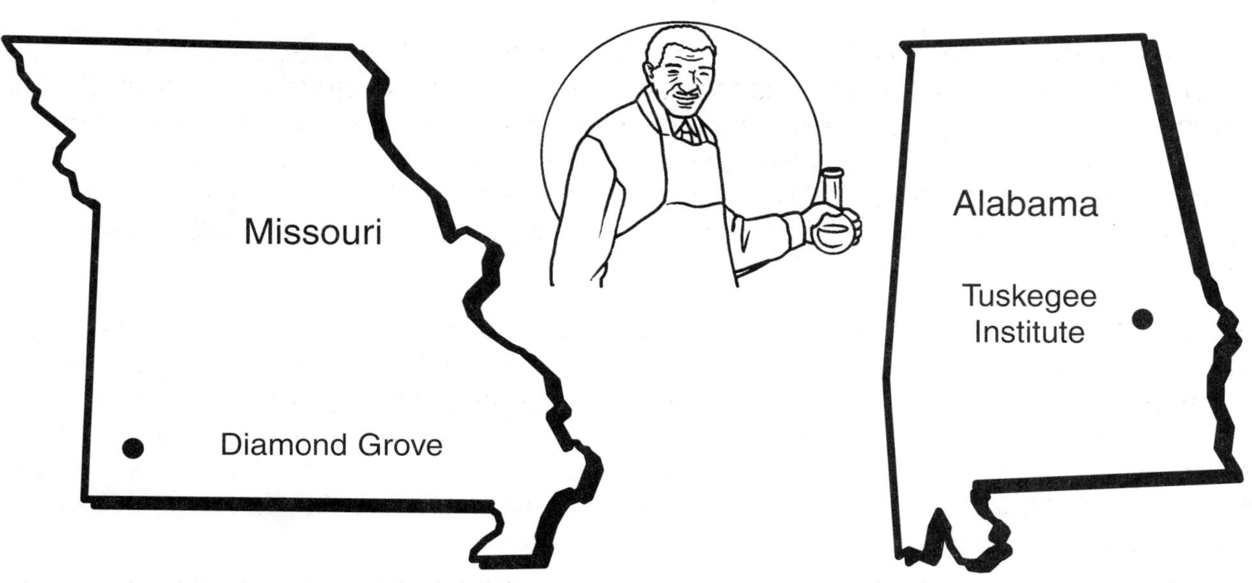

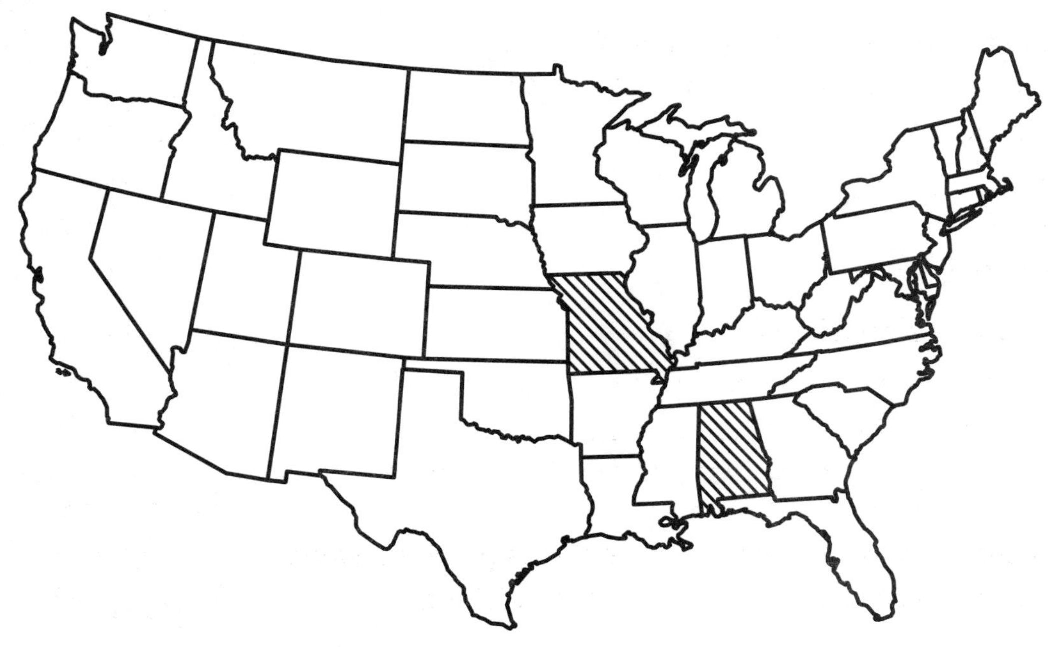

George Washington Carver was born on a plantation in Missouri.

1

George Washing Carver

1864–1943

He loved to learn and went to school when he could. In college, his teacher thought he should be a plant scientist. He became the first black professor at Iowa State University.

3

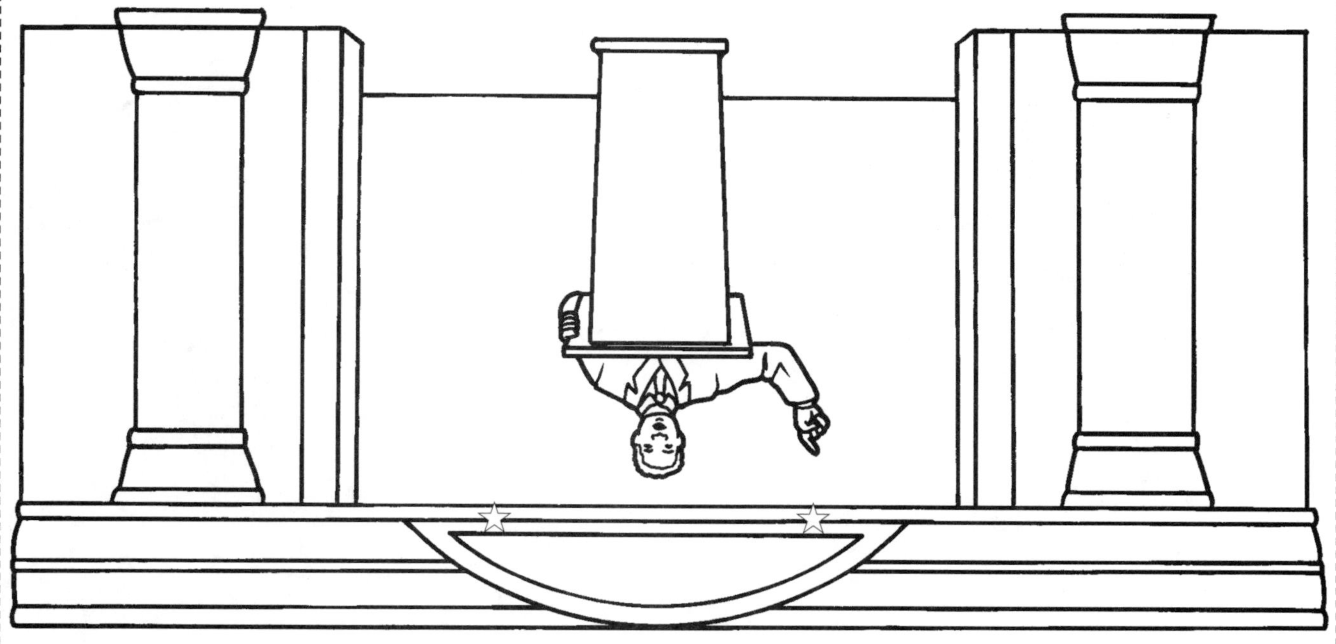

He loved plants, especially roses. As a young boy he became known to his neighbors as a "plant doctor." He also loved to paint pictures of flowers.

2

Carver liked to make things from peanuts, sweet potatoes, and other plants. He cared about soil and wanted to keep it healthy so a little land could yield a big harvest. 5

Dear George,

We need you here at Tuskegee Institute.
Please teach the students about soil and farming.

Sincerely,

Booker T. Washington

Booker T. Washington asked George Washington Carver to come to the Tuskegee Institute to teach students about nature and plants. 4

George Washington Carver

Lift tabs for *George Washington Carver*

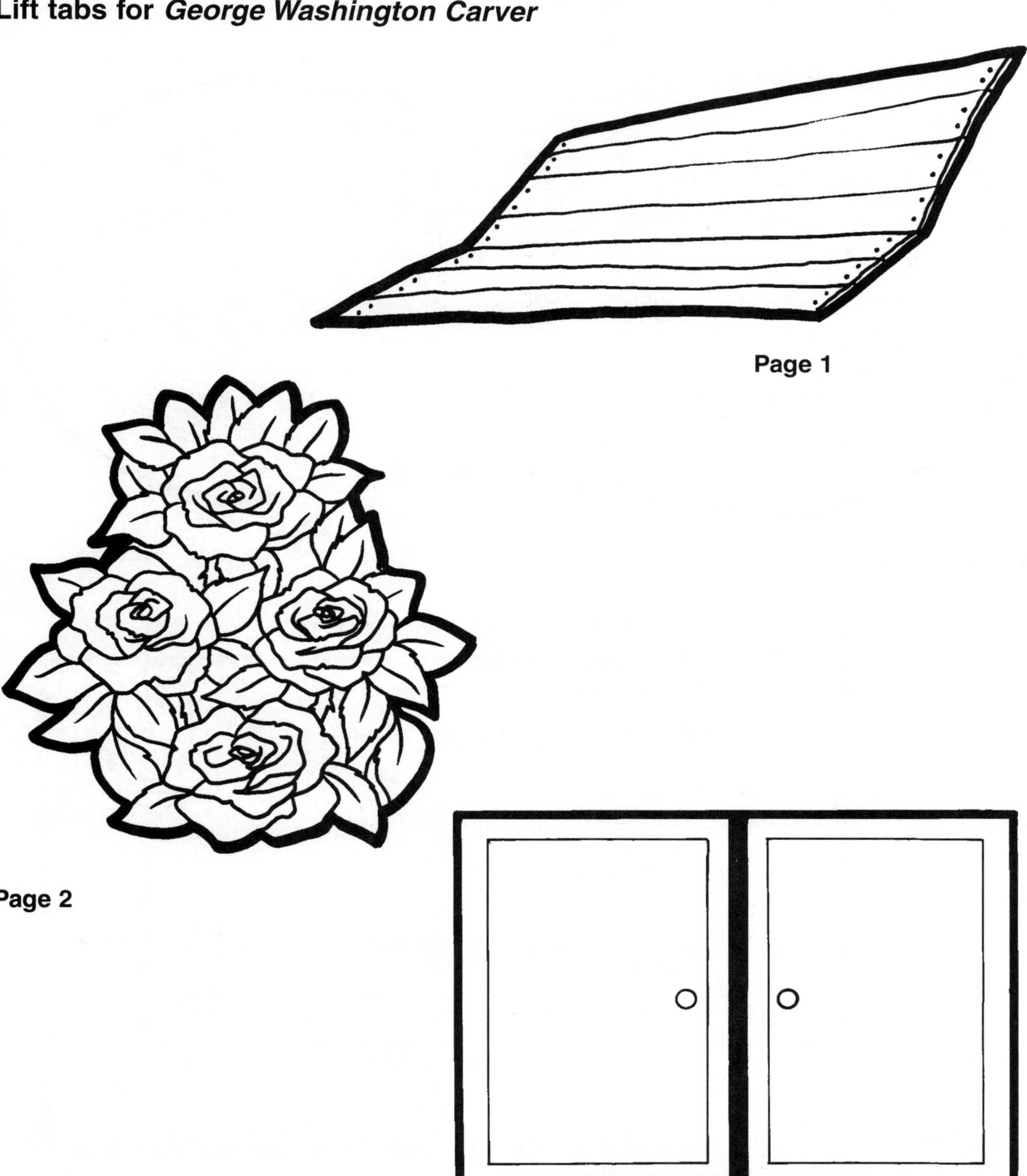

Page 1

Page 2

Page 3

George Washington Carver

Lift Tabs for *George Washington Carver* *(cont.)*

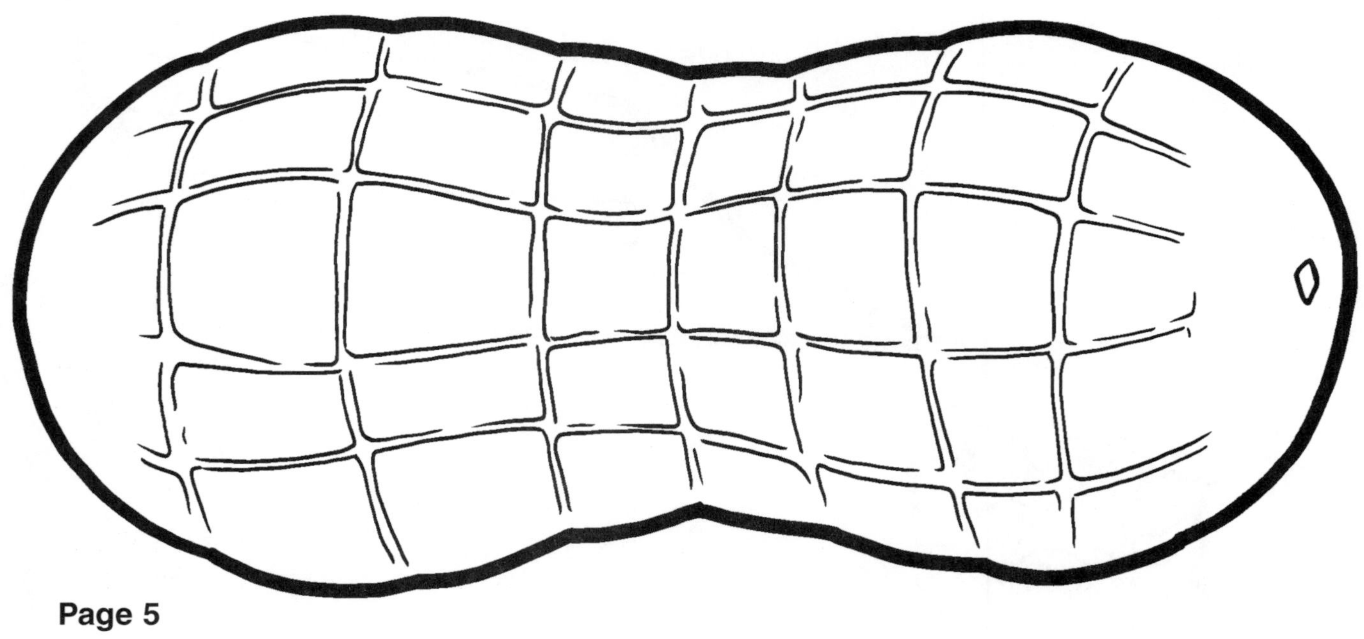

Page 5

Booker T. Washington
Tuskegee Institute, AL

George Washington Carver
Iowa State University
Iowa

Page 4

Martin Luther King, Jr.

The Emancipation Proclamation signed by President Abraham Lincoln in 1863 gave freedom and equality to the African-Americans slaves in the United States. He wanted all people to be equal. Unfortunately, nearly 100 years later, conditions had not changed significantly in some parts of the country. Whites and blacks remained separate in many states. Many African Americans struggled and continue to struggle for true equality.

One of the most courageous advocates for equality was Dr. Martin Luther King, Jr. Dr. King. believed that he could help change the way people treated each other. In 1964 he said, "*We must learn to live together as brothers or perish together as fools*." He believed that equality could be achieved without violence.

Martin Luther King, Jr., was born in Atlanta, Georgia, in 1929. He was a good student and, at age 15, enrolled in Morehouse College in Atlanta where he decided to become a minister. He went on to get a doctorate in theology in 1955 at Boston University. While in Boston, he met Coretta Scott. They married and had four children. The family lived in Montgomery, Alabama, where Dr. King was pastor of the Dexter Avenue Baptist Church.

A wonderful and moving speaker, Dr. King spent his life persuading people to end discrimination. He led marches and peaceful demonstrations during the 1950s and 1960s, demanding equal rights for African Americans. His words and actions motivated millions of people and encouraged real change. Dr. King gave his eloquent, stirring "I Have a Dream" speech at a peaceful demonstration he helped organize in 1963, called the March on Washington.

"I have a dream that one day ... the sons of former slaves and the sons of former slave owners will be able to sit down together at the table of brotherhood... I have a dream that my four little children will one day live in a nation where they will not be judged by the color of their skin but by the content of their character."

The Nobel Peace Prize was awarded to Dr. Martin Luther King, Jr., in 1964 for his work promoting peace. Sadly, not all people shared his belief or dream of equality for all. Martin Luther King, Jr., was killed by an assassin on April 4, 1968. He was only 39 years old.

On the third Monday of January each year, the people of the United States honor him for his courage, his words, and his dream. His wife and children continue the work he started. His message that goals can be reached with dignity and love through nonviolence still lives today.

Martin Luther King, Jr.

Map Study

Martin Luther King, Jr., was born in Atlanta, Georgia. He was a minister and a civil rights activist in Montgomery, Alabama.

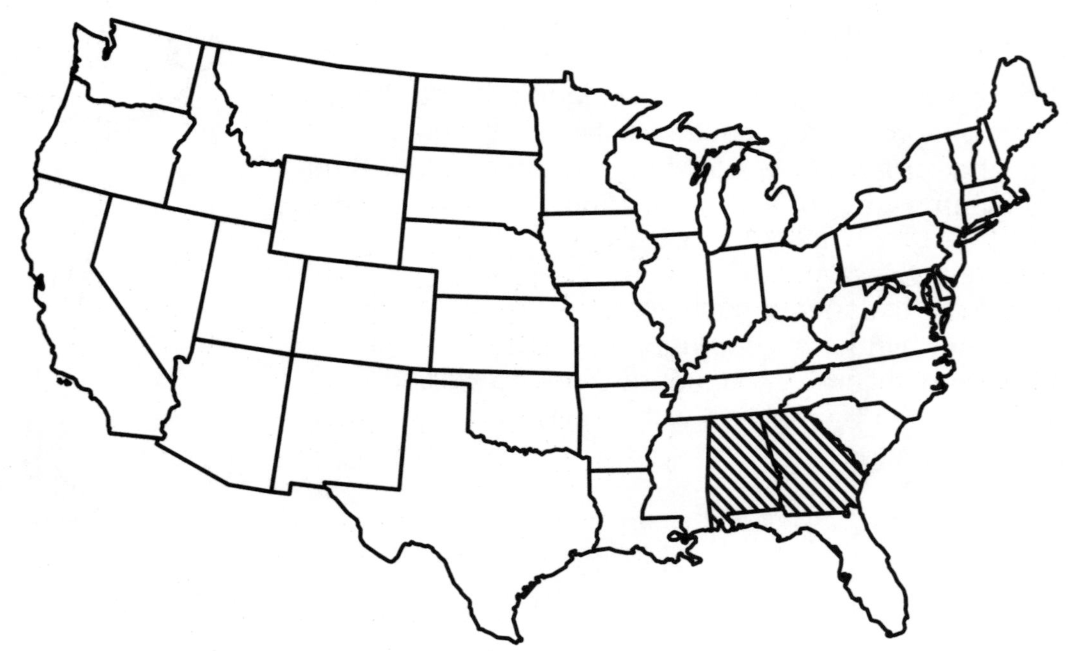

Putting Together *I Have a Dream*

Materials

- text pages
- tab pages
- scissors
- glue
- stapler
- markers or crayons

Assembly Directions for the *I Have a Dream* Lift-tab Book

1. Color the book pages.
2. Cut out the pages and put them in numerical order.

1 & 2

3. Staple the pages together on the left side.
4. Cut out the tabs.
5. Color the tabs to match the rest of the picture.

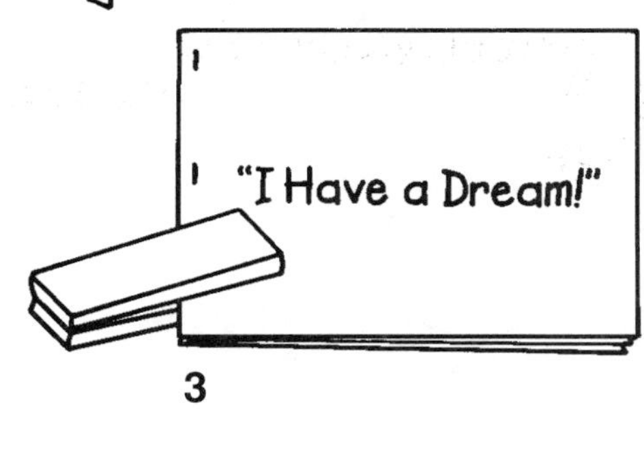

3

4

6. Place a dot of glue on each star. Attach the appropriate tab to the star.
7. Share the book with a friend.

6

"I Have a Dream!"

Martin Luther King, Jr., had a dream he shared with the American people.

He dreamed of a world where all people are treated with respect.

2

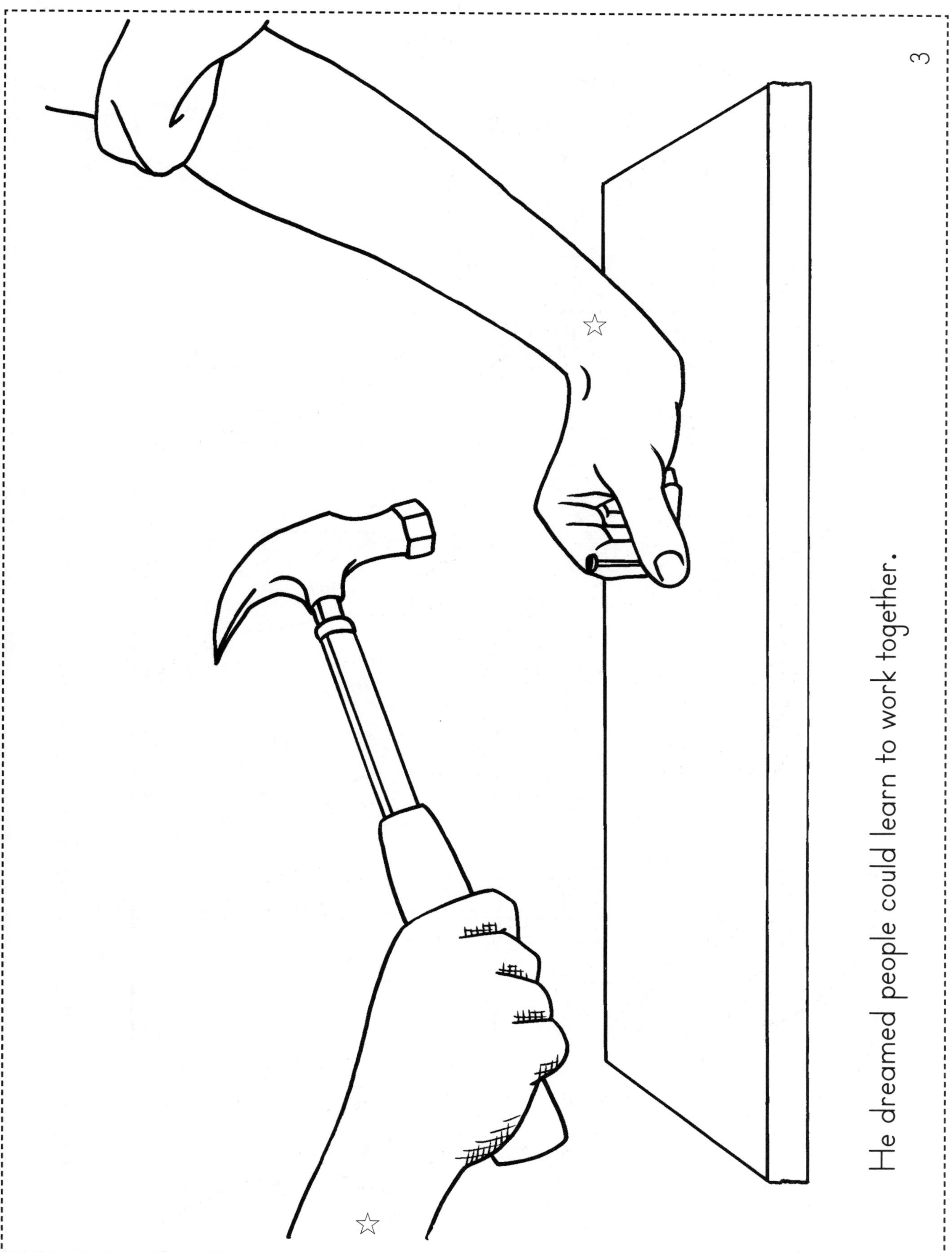
3
He dreamed people could learn to work together.

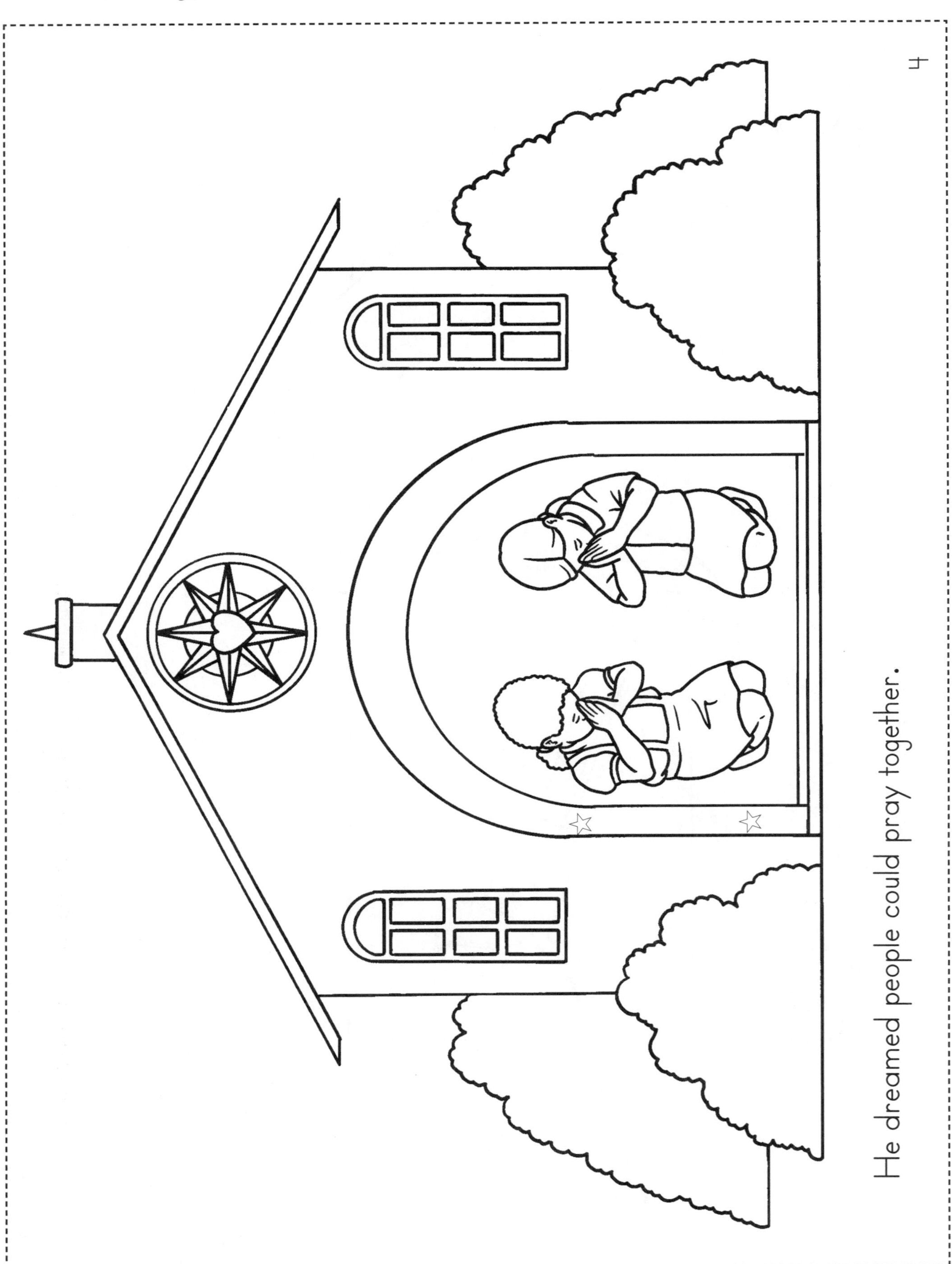
4
He dreamed people could pray together.

He dreamed people would stand up for freedom together.

5

6
He wanted all people to be free one day.

Martin Luther King, Jr.'s dream lives on today. What is your dream?

Martin Luther King, Jr.

Lift tabs

Martin Luther King, Jr. *(cont.)*

Lift tabs

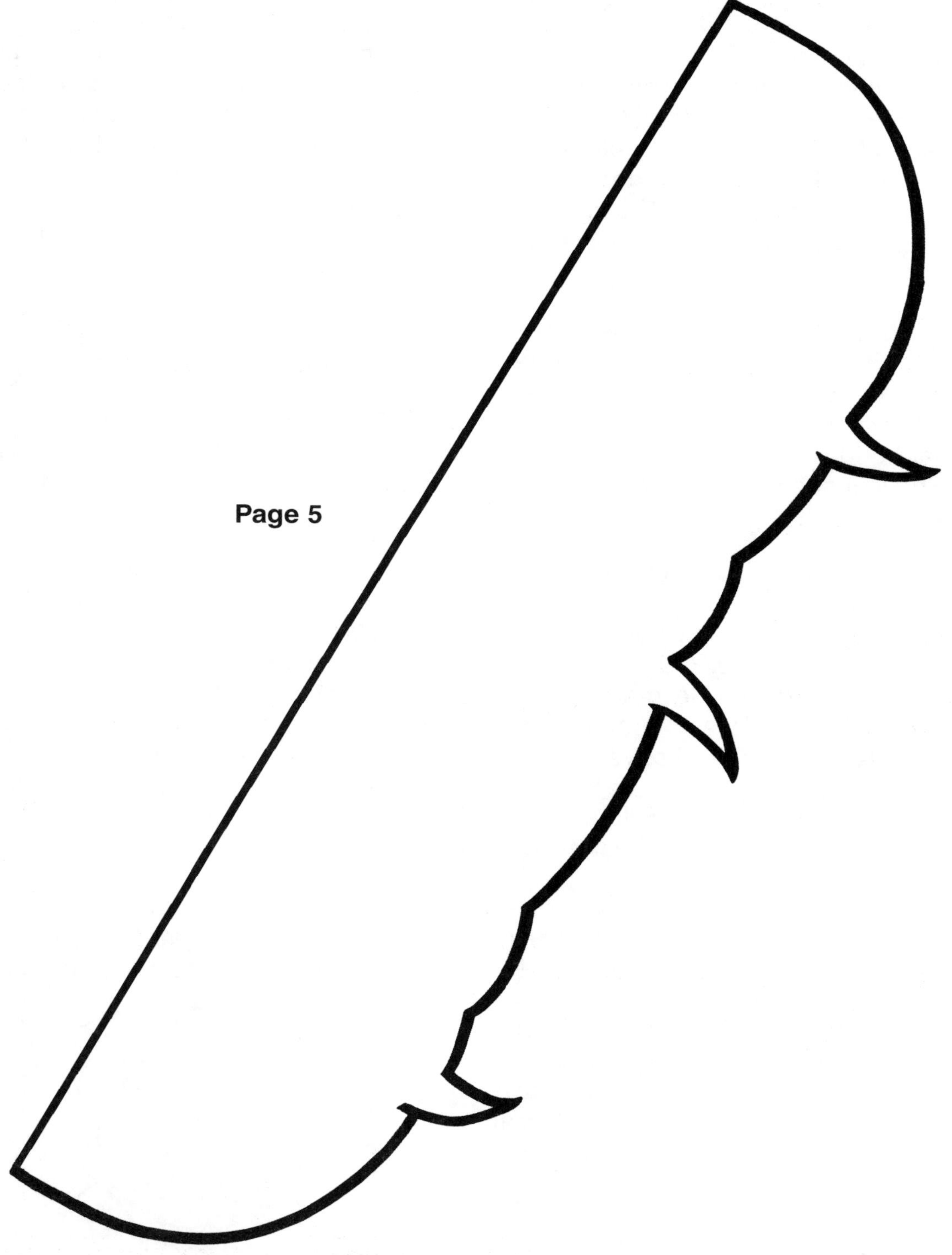

Harriet Tubman

Harriet Tubman was born a slave in Bucktown, Maryland around 1821. Because she was a slave, she was not allowed to go to school. Harriet had to work hard from the time she was very young. Harriet was a small person but was unusually strong and worked hard. In 1849, Harriet's master died and she learned that she and her family were to be sold to plantation owners farther to the south. She knew that conditions were even worse for slaves farther south and did not want to go. Harriet and her brothers decided to escape. They left their home in eastern Maryland in the middle of the night. Her brothers soon turned back, but Harriet kept going. She headed north alone. With the North Star as her guide, and assistance from the Underground Railroad, she finally reached Philadelphia, Pennsylvania. She worked as a laundress, a cook, and a seamstress. She wanted to save money to help her family.

Harriet was free in Philadelphia, but her friends and family were still in Maryland. She called herself a stranger in a strange land and wrote in her autobiography, "To this solemn resolution I came; I was free, and they should be free also; I would make a home for them in the North, and the Lord helping me, I would bring them all there." She did just what she set out to do, believing that freedom lay in the North. Over the next 12 years Harriet returned to the South 19 times. She is responsible for smuggling more than 300 people to freedom, including her elderly parents.

The Fugitive Slave Law of 1850 made it unsafe for runaway slaves to stay anywhere in the United States. It was against the law for a citizen to help a runaway slave reach freedom. Slaveowners could hire a bounty hunter to find the escaped slave and return him or her to the plantation. The fugitive slaves hid by day and traveled by night, often helped along the way by "agents" on the Underground Railroad. This "railroad" was neither underground, nor a railroad. The Underground Railroad was a group of people who worked to help slaves escape to freedom in the North. People who were against slavery hid fleeing slaves in their homes. They helped them get to the next safe place in spite of the dangers to themselves. Harriet, a "conductor" for the Underground Railroad, never lost a "passenger." Luckily, she was never captured herself despite there being a $40,000 reward for her return.

During the Civil War, Harriet served as a spy, a nurse, a cook, and a scout for the Union Army. She was able to move among the slaves behind Confederate lines and gather useful information for the North. She encouraged slaves to join the Union forces. She viewed her work as another way in which to fight against slavery.

After the war, Harriet Tubman continued to work to improve the lives of former slaves. On her own land, she opened a home for poor and elderly African Americans. She also worked with the women's movement and with the temperance movement. She died on March 10, 1913. She received full military honors at her funeral. In 1978, a Harriet Tubman stamp was issued in her honor.

Harriet Tubman

Map Study

Harriet Tubman led over 300 people to freedom on the Underground Railroad.

Putting Together *Harriet Tubman*

Materials

For each student you will need:

- copies of each sheet of text
- copies of the flaps
- scissors
- glue
- stapler
- markers or crayons

Assembly Directions for the *Harriet Tubman* Lift-tab Book

1. Color the pages.
2. Cut out the pages and put them in numerical order.
3. Staple the pages together on the left side.
4. Cut out the tabs.
5. Place a dot of glue on each star. Attach the appropriate tab.
6. Color the tabs to match the rest of the picture on the page.
7. Share the book with a friend.

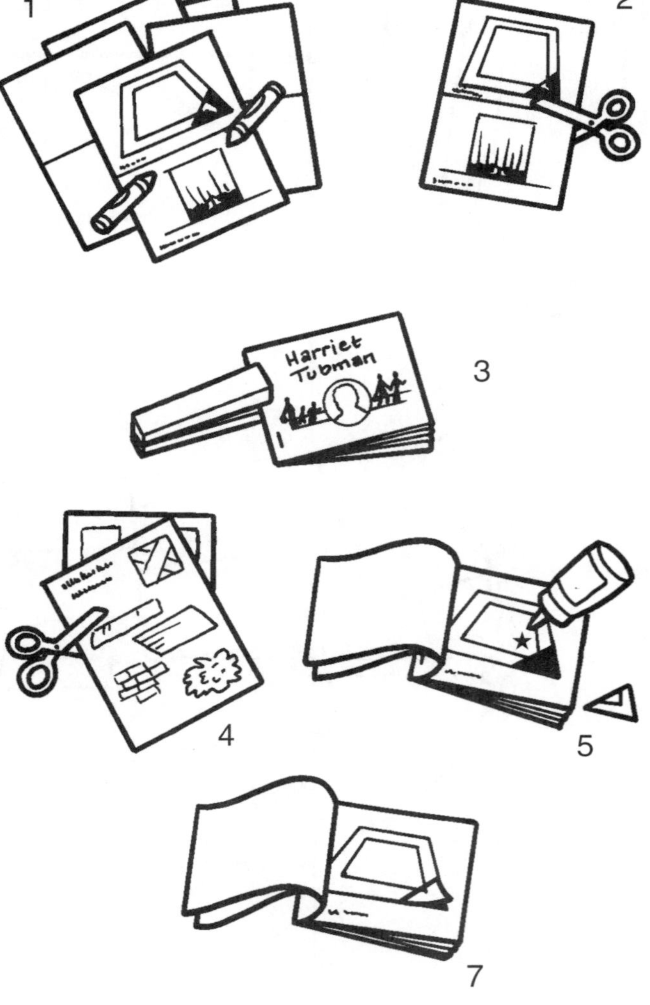

HARRIET TUBMAN

Harriet Tubman, I've been told;
'bout your Underground Railroad.
When my friends were scared and cried,
You helped them find a place to hide:

1

Under the floors,

2

Behind the doors,

3

Out in the shed

4

Under the bed.

5

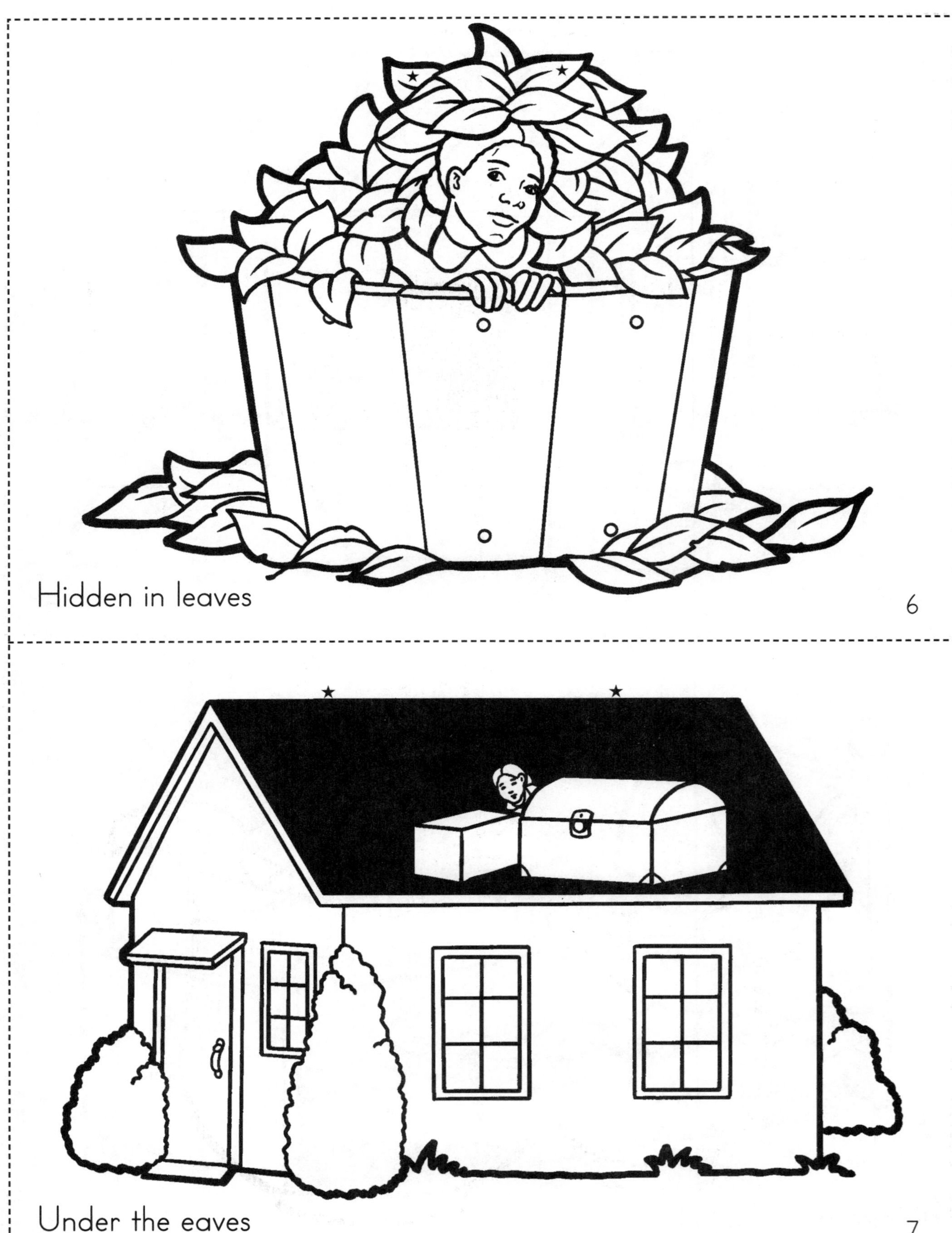

Hidden in leaves

6

Under the eaves

7

Behind the wall

8

Or plant in the hall

9

Harriet Tubman, please take me.
If I board I'll soon be free.
Headed North as slaves have strode
on your Underground Railroad!

10

Lift-tabs for *Harriet Tubman*

Page 3

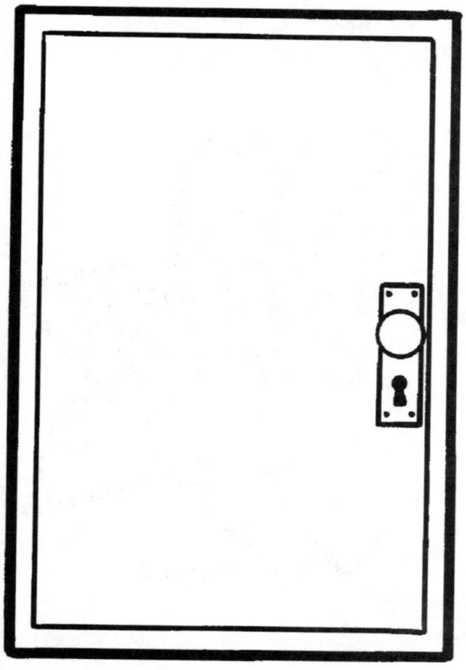

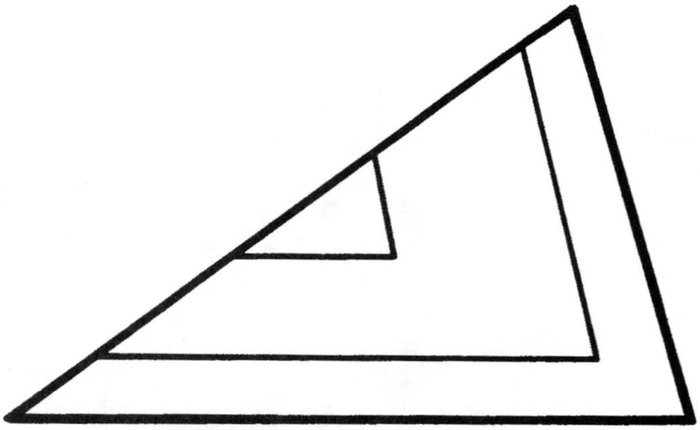

Page 2

Page 6

Harriet Tubman

Lift-tabs for *Harriet Tubman*

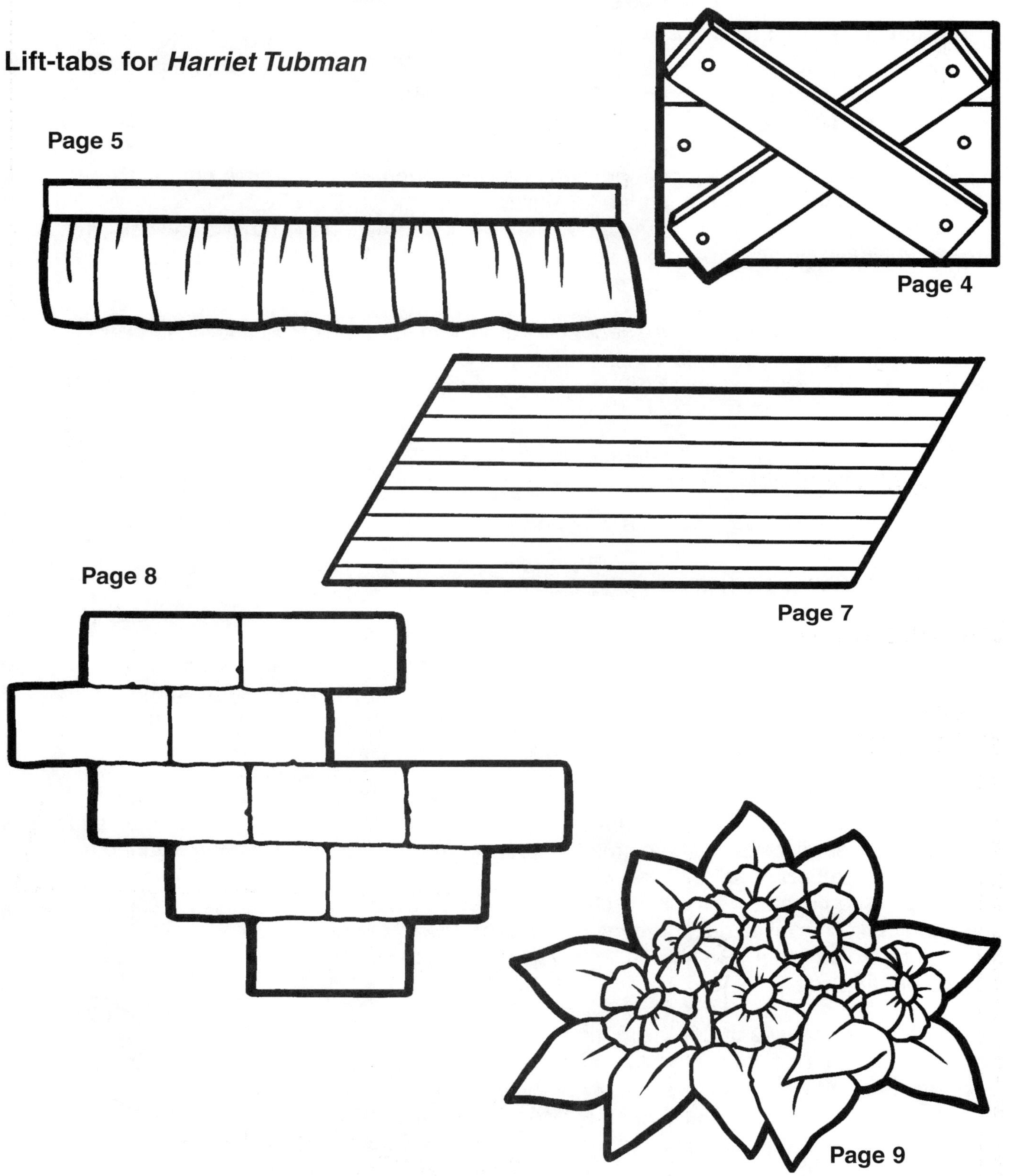

Benjamin Franklin

Benjamin Franklin was an author, a publisher, a statesman, and an inventor. His accomplishments are quite varied and remarkable in that, for the most part, he was self-taught. He was born in Boston on January 17, 1706. He had 16 brothers and sisters. At the age of ten, his father made him quit school and taught him to make soap and candles in his shop. Young Ben didn't like soap-making or candle-making, so his big brother taught him how to print. He became quite adept at printing and was soon ready to branch out on his own. He left Boston as a teenager and headed for Philadelphia, the largest city in the colonies. He worked for different printers before owning his own shop. Although Franklin had very little formal education, he was an excellent writer. He wrote many of the articles published in his newspaper, the *Philadelphia Gazette*.

One of his most famous books was *Poor Richard's Almanac*, which he published every year using the pen name Richard Saunders. It offered weather predictions, advice, jokes, and information of all sorts. It contained many sayings that are still in use today, including the following:

- "Early to bed, early to rise, makes a man healthy, wealthy, and wise."
- "Little strokes fell great oaks."
- "A penny saved is a penny earned."
- "A fool and his money are soon parted."
- "A stitch in time saves nine."
- "An apple a day keeps the doctor away."

Mr. Franklin was instrumental in the growth of Philadelphia, his chosen city. He started a more efficient post office, a road system, a subscription library, and a fire safety system. He also started a new hospital and a college. Philadelphia became an outstanding city in the colonies as a result of his contributions.

Franklin's inventions are significant and numerous as well. He created a more efficient heating stove, known as the Franklin stove, and more efficient eyeglasses, known as bifocals As a scientist, he discovered the connection between electricity and lightning. During a thunderstorm he flew a metal-tipped kite with a key attached to the string. When lightning struck, electricity traveled to the key, creating sparks. Franklin never patented any of his work. He did not wish to profit from it. He shared his inventions to make the world a better place.

As a statesman, he was the only American to sign all four of the following important documents in American history: The Declaration of Independence, the Treaty of Alliance with France, the Treaty of Peace with Great Britain, and the Constitution of the United States. As an ambassador in France and Great Britain, he helped to create better relations with these countries. He died at the age of 84 in Philadelphia. He lived a full, creative life and added greatly to the growth of his country.

Benjamin Franklin

Map Study

Ben Franklin spent most of his life in Philadelphia, Pennsylvania.

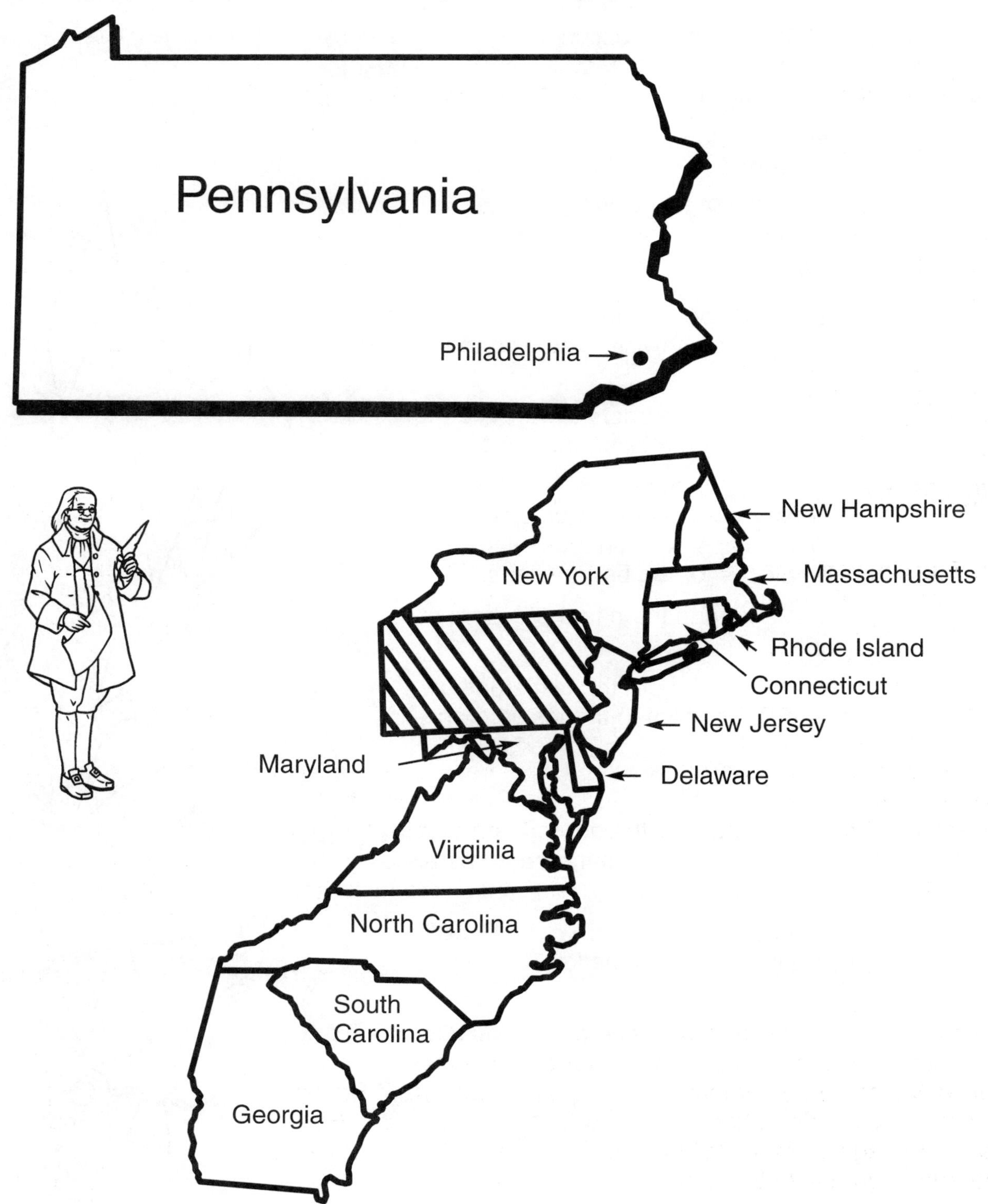

Putting Together *Benjamin Franklin*

Materials

- One piece of 9" x 12" construction paper, any color
- a 24" piece of string
- a 4" x 6" piece of yellow or gray construction paper
- three 2" x 5" pieces of any color construction paper
- a copy of titles and text
- stapler
- glue and cellophane tape
- scissors

Assembly Directions

1. To make the kite shape, fold the 9" x 12" sheet of construction paper lengthwise, matching the ends. Unfold.
2. Diagonally fold both top corners toward the center line of the paper, making the ends meet.
3. Use a straight edge to draw lines from the center point at the bottom to the bottom outside corners of the folded, top flaps. Cut on these lines, reserving the pieces for the bottom flaps.
4. Flip the pieces and tape them to the bottom of the kite shape.
5. Unfold all four flaps. Cut out the text strips on dotted lines and glue them to the inside of the kite.
6. Fold the flaps back over.
7. Cut out the titles and glue the appropriate one to the front of each flap. (Make sure the numerals correspond.)
8. Cut out and trace the key pattern onto 4" x 6" construction paper. Cut out the key, then cut out and attach the title.
9. Cut out the bow pattern. Trace onto three 2" x 5" pieces of construction paper. Cut out the bows.
10. Make the kite tail by taping the string to the back of the kite. Tape the key and the bows down its length.

Benjamin Franklin

Left Side of Kite

Interior

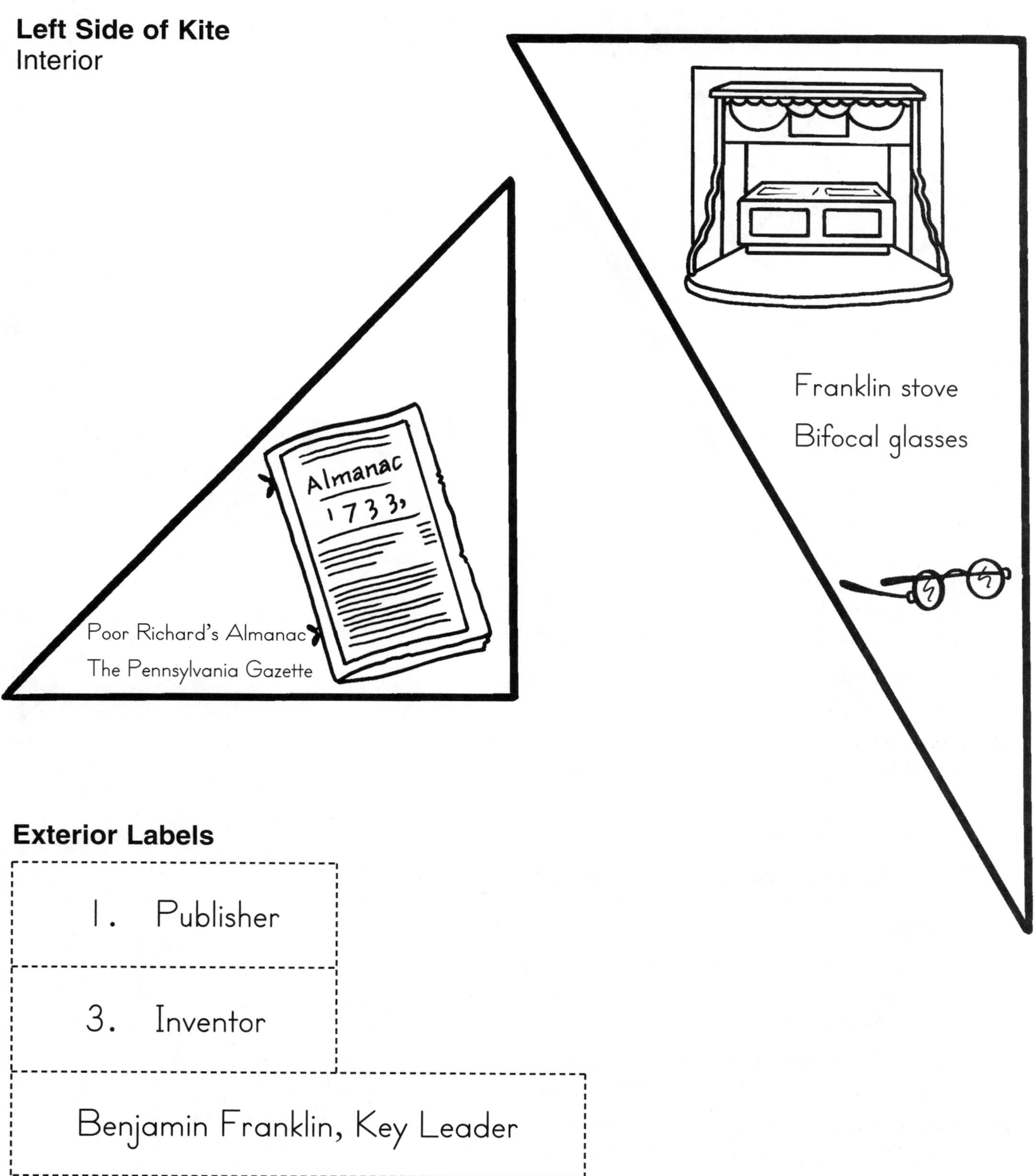

Exterior Labels

1. Publisher

3. Inventor

Benjamin Franklin, Key Leader

Benjamin Franklin

Right Side of Kite

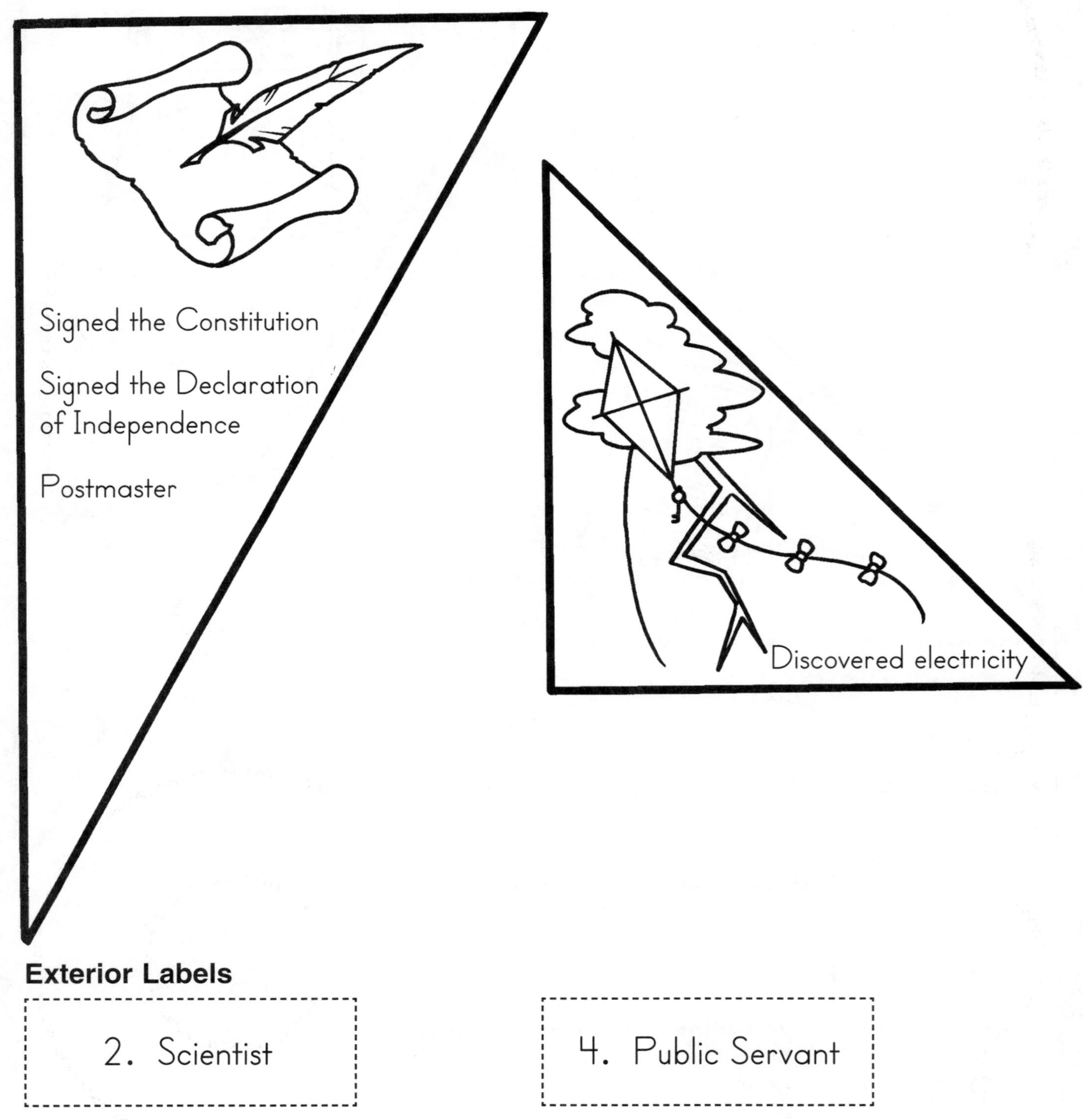

Exterior Labels

2. Scientist

4. Public Servant

Benjamin Franklin

TEMPLATES FOR KEY AND BOWS

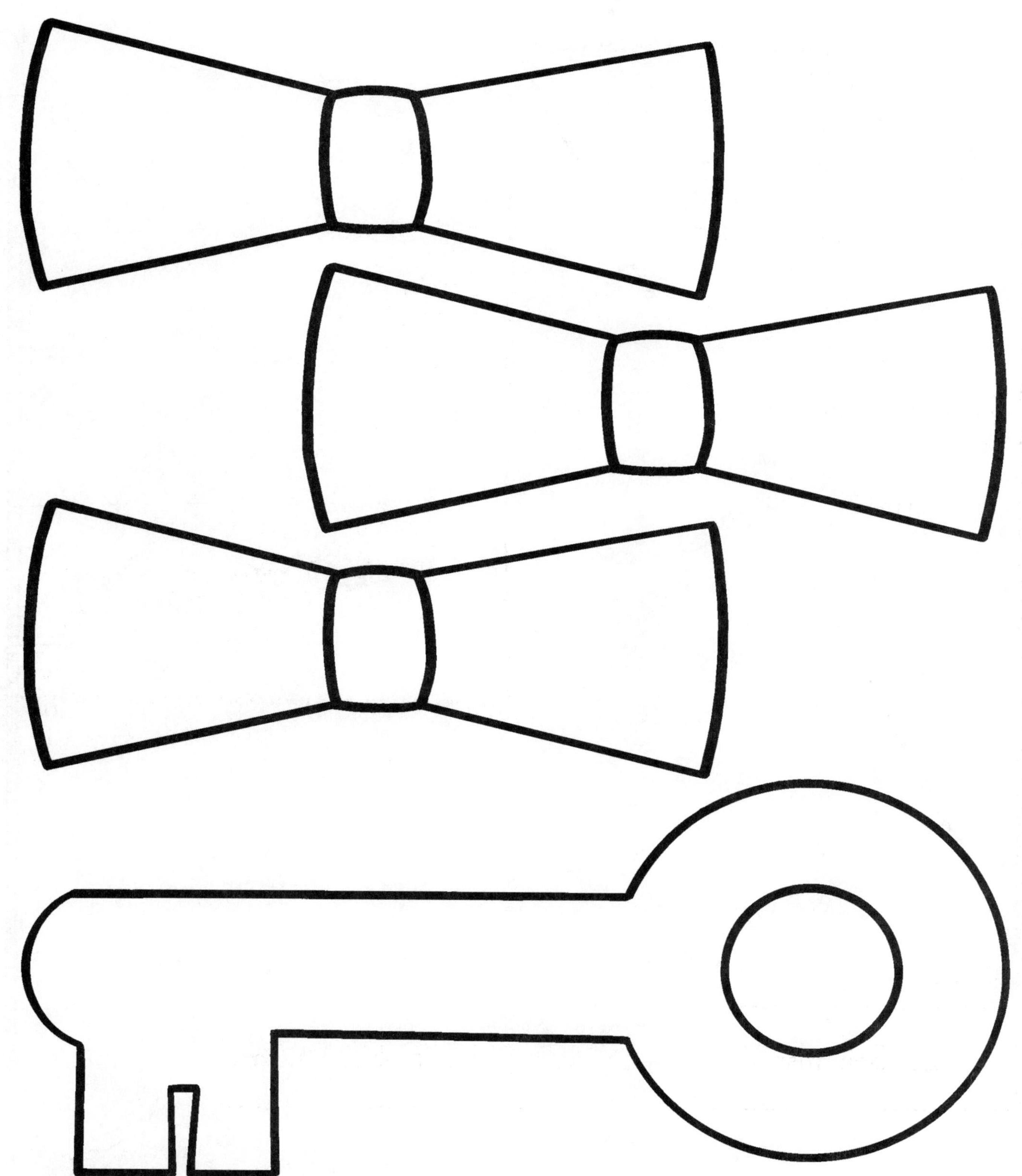

Map of the United States

Map of the United States

Map of the United States

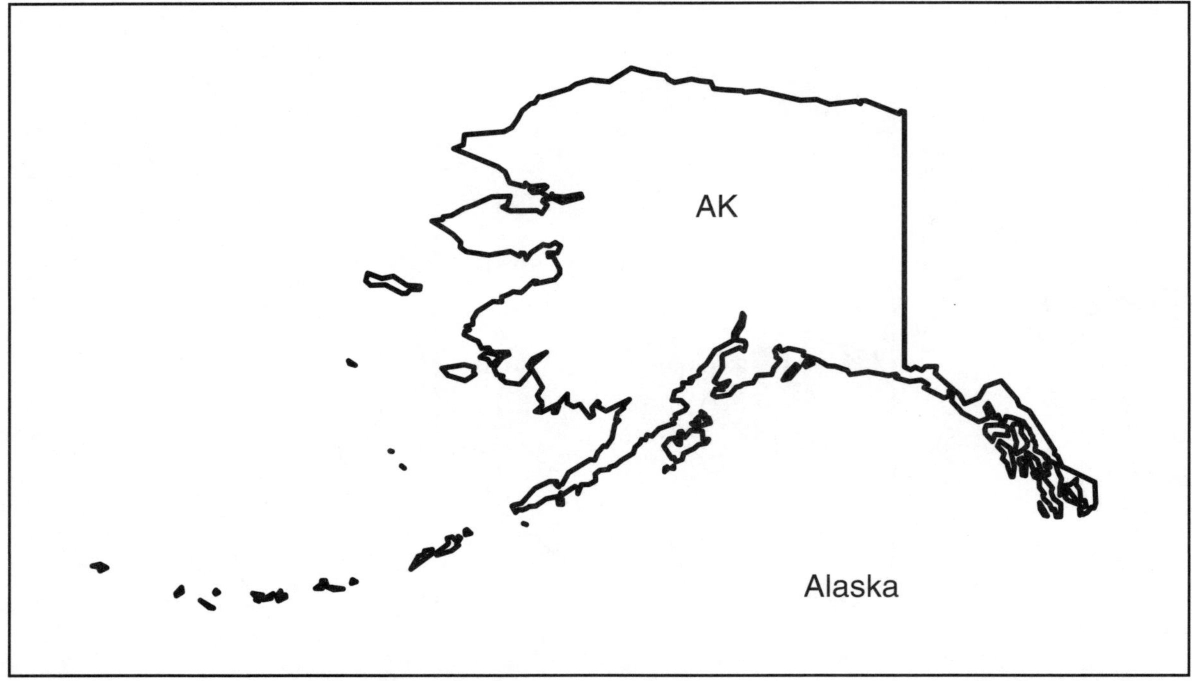

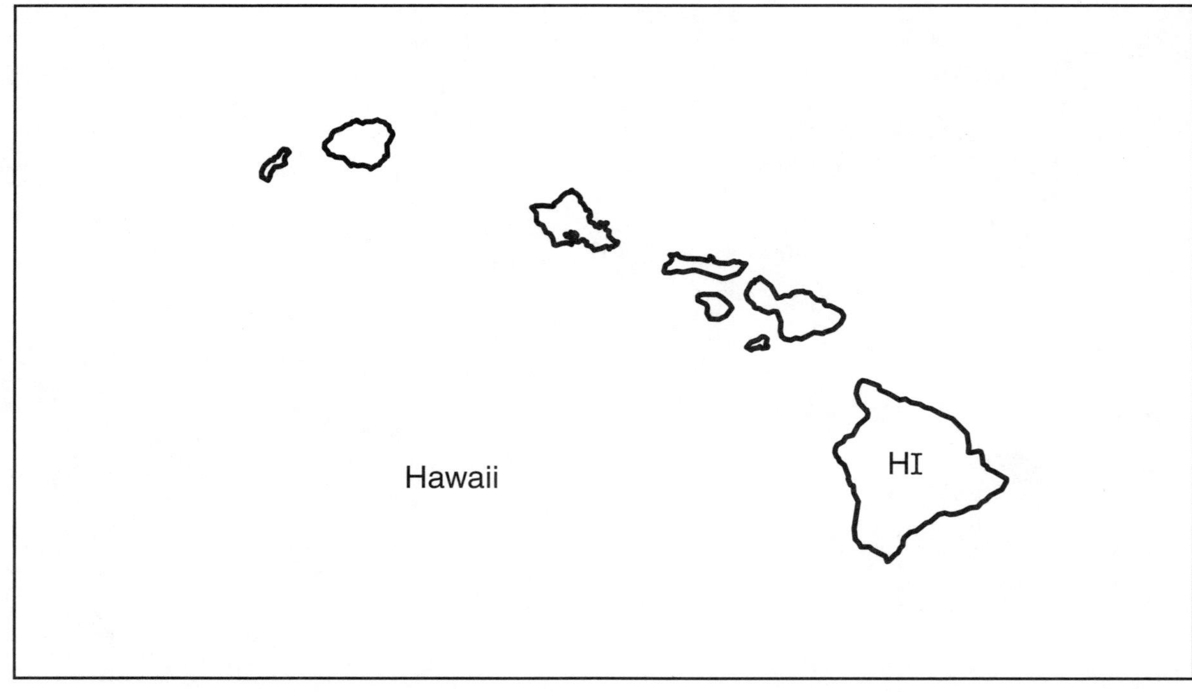